P9-CZV-087

William J. Fray

JOSEPH A. FITZMYER, S.J.

A
Christological
Catechism

NEW TESTAMENT
ANSWERS

NEW REVISED AND
EXPANDED EDITION

PAULIST PRESS *New York / Mahwah*

1991

IMPRIMI POTEST
Rev. Eduardus Glynn, S.J.
Praepositus Provinciae Marylandiae

NIHIL OBSTAT
Rev. Stephen J. Brett, S.S.J.
Censor Deputatus

IMPRIMATUR
Rev. William J. Kane
Vicar General for the Archdiocese of Washington

November 13, 1990

The *nihil obstat* and *imprimatur* are official declarations that a book or pamphlet is free of doctrinal or moral error. No implication is contained therein that those who have granted the *nihil obstat* and the *imprimatur* agree with the content, opinions, or statements expressed.

Copyright © 1991 by
The Corporation of the Roman Catholic Clergymen, Maryland.

All rights reserved. No part of this book may be reproduced or transmitted in any form or by any means, electronic or mechanical, including photocopying, recording, or by any information storage and retrieval system without permission in writing from the Publisher.

Fitzmyer, Joseph A.
    A Christological catechism: New Testament answers/ by Joseph A. Fitzmyer.
    —2nd ed.
        p.   cm.
    Includes bibliographical references and indexes.
    ISBN 0-8091-3253-2 (pbk.)
    1. Bible. N.T. Gospels—Criticism, interpretation, etc.   2. Jesus Christ—History of doctrines—Early church, ca. 30–600.   3. Jesus Christ—Person and Offices.   I. Title.
    BS2555.2.F49   1991
    225.6'7—dc20   91-21329
                                                                            CIP

Published by Paulist Press
997 Macarthur Boulevard
Mahwah, NJ 07430

Printed and bound in the United States of America

CONTENTS

ABBREVIATIONS

AAS	Acta Apostolicae Sedis		Enchiridion
AER	American Ecclesiastical Review		symbolorum (33d ed.; Freiburg im B.: Herder, 1965)
Ang	Angelicum		
Anton	Antonianum	EnchBib	Enchiridion biblicum:
ASS	Acta Sanctae Sedis		Documenta
BenMon	Benediktinische Monatschrift		ecclesiastica Sacram Scripturam spectantia
BeO	Bibbia e Oriente		auctoritate Pontificiae
BKirche	Bibel und Kirche		Commissionis de re
BLit	Bibel und Liturgie		biblica edita (2d ed.;
BTB	Biblical Theology Bulletin		Naples: M. D'Auria; Rome: A. Arnodo,
BZ	Biblische Zeitschrift		1954; 4th ed., 1961)
CBQ	Catholic Biblical Quarterly	HeyJ	Heythrop Journal
		HPR	Homiletic and Pastoral Review
ChicStud	Chicago Studies		
CivC	Civiltà Cattolica	HSNTA	E. Hennecke and W.
CJT	Canadian Journal of Theology		Schneemelcher (eds.), New Testament
ColBG	Collationes brugenses et gandavenses		Apocrypha (2 vols.; London: Lutterworth, 1963, 1965)
CSEL	Corpus scriptorum ecclesiasticorum latinorum	HTR	Harvard Theological Review
DaS	Divino afflante Spiritu	IER	Irish Ecclesiastical Record
DBSup	Dictionnaire de la Bible, Supplément (ed. L. Pirot et al.; Paris: Letouzey et Ané, 1928–)	ITQ	Irish Theological Quarterly
		LTK	Lexikon für Theologie und Kirche (11 vols.; 2d ed.; ed. J. Höfer and
DS	H. Denzinger and A. Schönmetzer,		

	K. Rahner; Freiburg im B.: Herder, 1957–67)	*RB*	*Revue biblique*
NCE	*New Catholic Encyclopedia* (15 vols.; New York: McGraw-Hill, 1967)	*RDiocNam*	*Revue diocésaine de Namur*
		RevistB	*Revista bíblica* (Argentina)
Nestle-Aland[26]	E. and E. Nestle and K. Aland, *Novum Testamentum graece* (26th ed.; Stuttgart: Deutsche Bibelstiftung, 1979)	*RSS*	*Rome and the Study of Scripture: A Collection of Papal Enactments on the Study of Holy Scripture with the Decisions of the Biblical Commission* (7th ed.; St. Meinrad, IN: Grail, 1962)
NHLE	*The Nag Hammadi Library in English* (ed. R. Smith; San Francisco, CA: Harper & Row; Leiden: Brill, 1988)		
		par.	parallel(s)
		SalTer	*Sal Terrae*
NJBC	*The New Jerome Biblical Commentary* (ed. R. E. Brown et al.; Englewood Cliffs, NJ: Prentice Hall, 1990)	SBLMS	Society of Biblical Literature Monograph Series
		ScCatt	*Scuola cattolica*
		Scr	*Scripture*
		SdZ	*Stimmen der Zeit*
NRT	*La Nouvelle Revue Théologique*	*TBT*	*The Bible Today*
ns	new series	*TheolGeg*	*Theologie der Gegenwart*
NTS	*New Testament Studies*	*TPQ*	*Theologisch-praktische Quartalschrift*
OssRom	*Osservatore Romano*		
pace	with all due respect to the opinion(s) of . . .	*TRev*	*Theologische Revue*
PG	*Patrologia graeca* (ed. J. Migne)	*TS*	*Theological Studies*
		ZAW	*Zeitschrift für die alttestamentliche Wissenschaft*
PL	*Patrologia latina* (ed. J. Migne)		

Praesidi magistrisque
Collegii Sanctae Crucis Vigorniensis
summo honore Litterarum Doctoris A.D. MCMLXXIX accepto

et

praesidi magistrisque
Universitatis Scrantoniensis
summo honore Doctoris Litterarum Humaniorum eodem anno
accepto
grato animo dedicatum

FOREWORD

Some years ago the director of *Chicago Studies* asked me to prepare a brief survey of New Testament christological problems for his "Pastoral Guide to the Bible."[1] It was simply entitled "Jesus the Lord" and proposed succinct answers to fifteen questions which the director had sent to me.

The entire pastoral guide was eventually translated into Italian under the title *Catechismo biblico.*[2] Later on, the director of *La Nouvelle Revue Théologique* requested that the article be updated and revised for a French version, to which request I was happy to accede.[3] The French form of the article included a further question (§7) and the reformulation of some answers to the original questions.

The text that was presented in the first edition of this book was a further improvement of the original English article. The wording of the answers was revised, and four new questions (§4, 8, 14, 15) were added, bringing the total to twenty. The new questions were suggested by readers of the French form of the article.[4] In this second

---

1. *ChicStud* 17 (1978) 75–104.

2. Ed. George J. Dyer (Brescia: Queriniana, 1979).

3. "Nouveau Testament et christologie: Questions actuelles," *NRT* 103 (1981) 18–47, 187–208. This form of the article has appeared in Danish in *Magasin* 4–5 (1981) 3–66; an abridgement of it was also to appear in *TheolGeg* (1982).

4. The French form has since appeared in book-form, *Vingt questions sur Jésus-Christ* (Paris: Cerf, 1983) [not well translated, it also omits the appendix]; Spanish translation of the English book-form, *Catecismo cristológico: Respuestas del*

edition I have added five more questions (§3, 5, 9, 21, 25), questions that persons have asked me about since the book first appeared. Minor revisions of the formulation of both questions and answers have also been introduced at times. In all, my effort has been to update the discussion and make it more practical for readers in the last decade of this century.

The answer to one question (§4), however, touches on an issue which lies at the heart of the problems discussed in this book. For the catechism builds upon the Instruction of the Biblical Commission issued in 1964 on the historical truth of the gospels. Having written a commentary on that Instruction in the year that it was issued,[5] I have come to realize how pertinent that church document is to the present christological discussion. As a result, I included in the appendix a revised form of that commentary, a slightly revised form of the translation of the Instruction prepared in 1964, and the significant paragraph 19 of *Dei Verbum,* the Dogmatic Constitution on Divine Revelation from Vatican Council II, which made explicit use of the Instruction. In this way it will be seen that the answers given in this catechism to the questions proposed have been inspired

---

nuevo testamento (Salamanca: Sigueme, 1984); Italian translation, *Domande su Gesù: Le risposte del Nuovo Testamento* (Universale teologica 20; Brescia: Queriniana, 1987); Flemish translation, *Geloven in vraag en antwoord; De historische Jezus en de Christus van het Geloof volgens het Nieuwe Testament* (Antwerp/Amsterdam: Patmos, 1987); Lithuanian translation, *Raktiniai klausimai apie Kristu* (Putnam, CT: Krikšcionis Gyvenime, 1986).

5. Entitled, "The Biblical Commission's Instruction on the Historical Truth of the Gospels," *TS* 25 (1964) 386–408. A more popular discussion of the Instruction was published under the title, "The Gospel Truth: What the Recent Vatican Statement Means to Modern Catholic Biblical Scholars," *America* 110 (1964) 844–46. The *TS* article was eventually published as a pamphlet, *The Historical Truth of the Gospels (The 1964 Instruction of the Biblical Commission): With Commentary* (Glen Rock, NJ: Paulist, 1965). The two articles (from *TS* and *America*) were combined into a booklet in a German version, *Die Wahrheit der Evangelien* (Stuttgart: Katholisches Bibelwerk, 1965). It was chosen to be the No. 1 issue of a series that has recently passed the hundred mark, "Stuttgarter Bibelstudien." Additions made to that form of the article have been incorporated into the revision presented in the appendix.

by the work of the Biblical Commission and of the fathers of Vatican Council II.

If I stress this point, it is to clarify what I am about in this book. A moment's reflection will make it clear that tomes could be written in answer to each of the questions posed. Originally, my intention was, and it still is, to give a succinct, well-worked-out answer to each question, with a minimum of bibliographic references and within a limited amount of space. Readers are asked to take this feature into account and realize the implications of such a brief-answer format. The answers are frankly proposed as my own, but they are fashioned from the standpoint of modern Catholic New Testament study and of today's research. In this regard they have been especially guided by the Instruction of the Biblical Commission.

My intention, then, is to set forth the New Testament data as succinctly as I can. The limitation of the answers to such data implies no judgment about the endeavors of others, either of the magisterium, or of systematic theologians, or of patristic scholars, who might seek to answer the same questions about Jesus the Lord on the basis of other data. In this regard the reader, after having read this book, would do well to peruse the Declaration of the Sacred Congregation for the Doctrine of the Faith, *Mysterium Filii Dei,* on the incarnation and the blessed Trinity,[6] and above all the International Theological Commission's *Select Questions on Christology.*[7] In these two texts one will see how theologians, coping with data derived from beyond the New Testament, try to answer some similar questions. The most crucial question in this whole area of christology will always remain that about the consciousness of the Jesus of history, Jesus of Nazareth. The treatment of that question by the

6. See *AAS* 64 (1972) 237–41. An English translation of the Declaration can be found in *Origins* 1/2 (1972) 665–68; see also "Safeguarding Belief in the Incarnation and Trinity," *Catholic Mind* (June 1972) 61–64.

7. (Washington, D.C.: United States Catholic Conference, 1980). The Latin text can be found in *Gregorianum* 61 (1980) 609–32.

Theological Commission is highly significant.[8] It goes beyond the purpose of this book, however, to try to deal with it in detail, but comments will be made about it in various ways, as occasion offers.

It remains to express my thanks to various persons who have helped me in bringing this book to its completion. I am indebted, first of all, to the Rev. George J. Dyer, the director of *Chicago Studies,* who initially asked me to compose such answers to his questions in the Pastoral Guide and who has granted permission for this revision and expansion of the article. Second, to Dr. John J. Collins of University of Notre Dame, who—as I learned only subsequently—had no small hand in the formulation of the fifteen questions originally proposed. Third, to R.P. Bruno Clarot, S.J., who first brought the *Chicago Studies* article to the attention of the director of *NRT.* Fourth, to R.P.H. Jacobs, S.J., the director of *NRT,* who requested the revision of the text and thus provided the stimulus for further work on it (as well as to his translator). Fifth, to Raymond E. Brown, S.S., who was kind enough to send me comments on the revised form of the article. Lastly, to Lawrence E. Boadt, C.S.P., Donald F. Brophy, and other members of Paulist Press who have graciously accepted this revision of several articles and made it into a book for me.

Joseph A. Fitzmyer, S.J.
Professor Emeritus, Biblical Studies
The Catholic University of America
Washington, DC 20064
Resident at the Jesuit Community
Georgetown University
Washington, DC 20057

---

8. No attempt is made in this document to discuss the consciousness of the Jesus of history in the part of it that deals with the "knowledge of the person and work of Jesus Christ" (IA or IB); it is found rather in the section which develops "the teachings of the Council of Chalcedon and Constantinople III" (IIID), specifically in §6.1ff. The latter makes all sorts of references to the New Testament, but they are made from the systematic point of view, and hardly from the viewpoint adopted in this book.

QUESTIONS

1. Do the Gospel Stories Present an Accurate Factual Account of the Teaching and Deeds of Jesus of Nazareth?

The question is complicated, for it is asked by implication from the viewpoint of modern historical thinking (e.g. of the sort that would ask whether Julius Caesar really crossed the Rubicon or George Washington the Delaware River). From that point of view the only answer which can be given to the question is meager indeed.

a. The main reason for such an answer is that we have inherited in the New Testament four different stories that purport to tell us what Jesus said and did. Though they contain many details in which one finds agreement among them, there is also a considerable amount of disagreement. The differences between the synoptic gospels—Mark, Matthew, and Luke—and the Johannine gospel are notorious (e.g. Did Jesus go up to Jerusalem during his ministry only once, or several times? Was he put to death on Passover or on the eve of Passover?). Clearly, the Johannine gospel has been composed with a preoccupation that is not that of the question posed above, for its stated purpose is: "These things are written that you may *believe* that Jesus is the Christ, the Son of God, and that believing you *may have life in his name*" (20:31). Moreover, the Jesus of John's gospel does not speak as does the Jesus of the synoptics. The former uses long, solemn discourses, filled with symbolic language, "I am" formulas, and references to the Father, and has virtually no parables. Very few of the episodes of Jesus' ministry recorded in the fourth gospel parallel those of the synoptics. Apart from the account of Jesus' initial relation to John the Baptist (which itself differs in crucial details [cf. Jn 3:26; 4:2]), the cure of the son of a royal official in Capernaum (4:46–53), the multiplication of the loaves (6:5–13), the walking on the waters (6:16–21), and a few scattered details of lesser moment, there is scarcely any real parallelism in the Johannine account with the synoptics before the last days of Jesus in Jerusalem. (What a picture of Jesus we would have, if we had only the fourth gospel! Would we know much about the humanity of Jesus?)

b. Within the synoptic tradition itself there are many similarities, which one might be tempted to regard as the factual core. But here, too, there are numerous differences, and not a few of the divergences are of great significance when one inquires about an "accurate factual account." To cite but a few examples: There are the different stories in the infancy narratives of Matthew and Luke that defy harmonization; in the former the heavenly communication about the child to be born is made to Joseph, but in the latter to Mary. One cannot claim without further ado that it actually came to both of them. Again, how different are the stories in Matthew 2 from those in Luke 2. Consider the divergent form of Jesus' sayings about the prohibition of divorce (with or without an exception), the number of petitions in the Our Father (seven in the Matthean form, five in the Lucan), the number of beatitudes at the beginning of the sermon on the mount/plain (eight in Matthew, four in Luke), the problematic ending of Mark's gospel, which may have ended at 16:8, with an account of the discovery of the empty tomb, but with no appearances of the risen Christ. The upshot is that, when one considers the synoptic gospel stories from the viewpoint of accurate, factual recounting, they can scarcely be judged to be prime examples of such writing.

c. If one were to try to limit the actual account of what Jesus did and said to what is found to be in agreement in the four gospels, there are still problems. On the one hand, this would for the most part limit the discussion to the substance of the passion narratives (Jesus' "last supper" with his followers, his arrest, the trials, the crucifixion, death, and burial of Jesus, and the finding of the empty tomb). On the other hand, with the exception of a few other episodes in the ministry itself (e.g. Peter's confession of Jesus [recounted, indeed, in different forms; see §14 below]), the vast majority of the Jesus-tradition would be seen to be reflected in a form that is at once concordant and discordant.

d. Furthermore, the concordant similarity in the synoptic accounts of Jesus' ministry raises a further question about the independence of these reports one from the other, and then whether they are any more accurate or reliable than the Johannine account. No matter what theoretic solution one uses for the synoptic problem (the discordant concord of the gospels of Mark, Matthew, and Luke), there is scarcely anyone today who would deny the interdependence of the Marcan, Matthean, and Lucan gospels.

The most commonly used solution to the synoptic problem is the so-called two-document hypothesis or the modified two-source theory. The two documents used in the composition of the Lucan and Matthean gospels would have been Mark and "Q" (an abbreviation of the German word *Quelle,* "source," used to designate the Greek written source postulated for about two hundred and thirty verses common to Matthew and Luke and not found in Mark). The modified two-source theory accepts the same two sources but admits that Luke also had a private (written or oral) source, "L," and that Matthew had a similar source, "M." In either case, the dependence of the Matthean and Lucan gospels on the Marcan is admitted for a large bulk of the common material. If one were to prefer the solution proposed by the eighteenth century scholar J.J. Griesbach, according to which the Marcan gospel is an abridgement of the Matthean and Lucan gospels—a highly questionable solution—a similar dependence is at least implied. Other solutions proposed in this century by French interpreters, such as X. Léon-Dufour and M.-E. Boismard, are not free of some form of interdependence of these gospels. Only a naive fundamentalism would still insist on the synoptic gospels as products solely of independent oral transmission.

Yet if the agreements among the synoptics are explained by their interdependence, the differences among them reveal that they are not all factually accurate. An editorial hand, modifying or redacting the transmitted material, has been at work on them, and usually for reasons other than the concern of history.

e. No serious New Testament interpreter, however, would try today to maintain that the gospel stories about Jesus are fabrications out of whole cloth (*pace* J.M. Allegro, R. Augstein, and others). An historical tradition lies behind both the synoptics and John. The concern of the modern interpreter of these writings is, then, not so much the sorting out of how much in either tradition is factually accurate as the appreciating and understanding of the heritage about Jesus that is enshrined in them. Both the synoptic and the Johannine gospels incorporate an historical nucleus, but also a varying literary preoccupation, which must be respected.

f. The multiplicity of accounts in the early Christian heritage reveals that they were not composed for the mere purpose of recording facts about Jesus. Between the facts themselves and the composition of the accounts at least a generation of Christian preaching about him and of tradition about him, oral and written, had intervened. This preaching and tradition included a recollection of what Jesus did and said, but it could not help but be colored by hindsight, meditation, and faith in him as the risen Lord, a developing christology, and echoes of later church concerns, of church-synagogue con-

troversies, of missionary endeavors, and of persecution. Such phe-
nomena do not necessarily preclude accurate reporting, but the end-
products, being four in number and having different emphases,
scarcely give the impression that they were intentionally written to
be accurate, factual accounts. Those extrinsic factors have left at
times clear traces in the accounts and contribute to the impression
that they were written for quite other purposes, as even Luke 1:1–4
(with its stress on *asphaleia,* "assurance") or John 20:31 reveals.

2. How Much Can We Claim To Know About the Jesus of History?

The sources of our information about the Jesus of history are
limited. It might be well to stress that "the historical Jesus," i.e. what
modern historical investigation can recover about him, is only part
of the real portrait of "the Jesus of history." Jesus of Nazareth or the
real "Jesus of history" led a full life as a Palestinian Jew and said or
did many things to which modern historical investigation has no
access. What can be reconstructed about him paints the picture of
"the historical Jesus," but "the historical Jesus" cannot be simply
equated with "the Jesus of history."

In reconstructing the portrait of the "historical Jesus," modern
historians make use of limited sources: a few items in ancient extrabiblical writings, possibly some details in apocryphal gospels of later
date, isolated pieces of information in the New Testament writings
other than the canonical gospels, and what may be regarded as authentic historical traditions embedded in the canonical gospels
themselves.

a. One can almost count on the fingers of one hand the extrabiblical references to Jesus in ancient writings that are independent
of the New Testament. A few lines are devoted to "Christ," the
author of a "pernicious superstition," by the Roman historian Taci-
tus (A.D. 56[?]–116[?]), who tells of Christians related to the burn-

ing of Rome by the emperor Nero and of the execution of Christ under the "procurator" Pontius Pilate, while Tiberius was emperor (*Annales* 15.44,3).

Suetonius (A.D. 69[?]–?) further tells of the expulsion of Jews from Rome ca. A.D. 49 by the emperor Claudius because of a tumult [between Jews and Jewish Christians?] instigated by "Chrestus" (probably to be understood as *Christus* because of itacism [the tendency of the time to pronounce Greek $\bar{e}$ as *iota*] working in reverse) (*Vita Claudii* 25.4).

The *Testimonium Flavianum* in the writings of the Jewish historian Flavius Josephus (A.D. 38–100[?]) speaks of Jesus as "a wise man, if indeed one ought to call him a man" and as one put to death by Pilate, "having heard him accused by men of the highest standing among us" (*Ant.* 18.3,3 §63–64 [written ca. A.D. 93–94]). But that testimony is widely suspected of being at least partly interpolated by Christian glossators of the manuscripts of Josephus, if not wholly so. Yet another passage (*Ant.* 20.9,1 §200), scarcely interpolated, tells of the putting to death of James, "the brother of Jesus called the Christ."

Again, Pliny the Younger (A.D. 61–112) knows that Christians of his day in Bithynia (Asia Minor) chanted verses "to Christ, as if to a god" (*Christo quasi deo*, in *Ep.* 10.96,7).

Lucian of Samosata, a traveling lecturer and Sophist rhetor (A.D. 120–180[?]), writes about the death of Peregrinus, a Cynic philosopher, who became a Christian for a while before reverting to Cynicism. For a time he associated with "the priests and scribes" of the Christians of Palestine, "interpreted and explained some of their books," and was revered by them "next after that other, to be sure, whom they still worship, the man who was crucified in Palestine because he introduced this new cult into (human) life" (*De morte Peregrini* 11). Lucian also speaks of Jesus as the "first lawgiver" of the Christians who "persuaded them that they all are brothers of one another" (an allusion to Matthew 23:8?) and refers to them as "wor-

shiping that crucified sophist himself and living under his laws"
(ibid. 13).

Finally, a baraita (an "outside" addition to the Mishnaic tradition) in the Babylonian Talmud (*Sanhedrin* 43a [third century at the earliest]) speaks of Yeshu, who practiced magic and led Israel into apostasy, had disciples, and was "hanged on the eve of Passover."

These extrabiblical texts are problematic, at times cryptic, at times allusive, at times interpolated. Yet even when due allowance is made for such problems in them, these extrabiblical references, independent of the New Testament writings, support at most a few details known mainly from the passion narratives of the canonical gospels: that Jesus was put to death in the reign of Tiberius under Pontius Pilate, that some leaders of the Palestinian Jews of his time were involved in his death, and that he had some followers by whom he was regarded as "Christ," lawgiver, founder of a new way of life, and "quasi deo."

   b. The apocryphal *Gospel according to Thomas,* extant in a fourth century Coptic version (see J.M. Robinson [dir.], *The Nag Hammadi Library in English* [3d ed.; San Francisco: Harper & Row; Leiden: Brill, 1988] 124–38) and in a few Greek fragments of the second/third century (see my *Essays on the Semitic Background of the New Testament* [London: Chapman, 1971; reprinted, Missoula, Mt.: Scholars, 1974] 355–433), ascribes to Jesus one hundred and fourteen sayings, usually introduced simply by "Jesus said." Most of these sayings, loosely strung together, actually come from a later date than that of the canonical gospels and depend on the latter. At times their gnostic concerns and reformulations betray the matrix in which they took shape. But this apocryphal gospel preserves some sayings or parables in a form that is more primitive than that found in the canonical gospels, i.e. devoid of editorial additions which almost certainly reflect the concerns of the evangelists (compare logion 64 with Mt 22:1–14 and Lk 14:16–24). But does "more primitive" necessarily mean "authentic"? It is not impossible, but who can say for sure?

c. Within the New Testament itself, yet outside of the gospel tradition, we find details about the earthly life and ministry of Jesus that are clearly independent of this tradition, having been composed prior to it at times. (I prescind from what is found in the Acts of the Apostles, because much of the detail in it may simply be echoing Luke's first volume.) In the genuine Pauline corpus, composed prior to the earliest gospel (Mark), we learn not only of the primitive kerygma about Jesus' death, burial, resurrection, and appearances as risen Lord (1 Cor 15:3–5), but also about his "last supper" with his disciples and of the institution of the eucharist "on the night he was betrayed" (1 Cor 11:23–25), of his "sufferings" (Phil 3:10), of his "cross" (1 Cor 1:17–18; Phil 2:8), of his "crucifixion" (Gal 2:20; 3:1; 1 Cor 1:23), of his "death" (1 Thess 5:10; 1 Cor 11:26; Rom 6:3), and of his "burial" (1 Cor 15:4; Rom 6:4). Allusion is also made to the crucifixion as his being "hung on a tree" (Gal 3:13). In his severe indictment of his former co-religionists, Paul speaks of "the Jews who killed the Lord Jesus" (1 Thess 2:14–15). Paul also knows of some sayings of Jesus, about the prohibition of divorce (1 Cor 7:10–11), about the eucharist (1 Cor 11:23–25), and about the *eschaton* (1 Thess 4:15).

In the possibly deutero-Pauline letter to the Colossians, allusion is made to Jesus being "nailed" to the cross (2:14). In the pseudepigraphic first letter to Timothy mention is made of Jesus' appearance before Pilate (6:13). See further 1 Pet 2:24 (cf. Acts 5:30; 10:39; 13:29); Heb 6:6; 13:12. Again, what is striking in these extra-evangelical references is the amount of detail that supports mainly details of the canonical passion narratives, but little of the rest of the story about Jesus (save perhaps a few of his sayings; see further D.L. Dungan, *The Sayings of Jesus in the Churches of Paul* [Philadelphia: Fortress, 1971]).

d. When one considers the things recorded in the canonical gospels about Jesus' sayings and deeds, one has to recall what was

said about these New Testament writings in §1 above: that their
purpose was quite other than that of an accurate factual account.
Being primarily testimonies of faith and propaganda for faith, they
do not pretend to give us per se a factual sketch of the earthly life and
ministry of Jesus of Nazareth. Nothing is really said in them about
his physical appearance or his customary habits, or even about his
historical consciousness. Being composed at least a generation after
his death, the canonical gospels cannot be regarded as first-hand
evidence of his consciousness or first-hand reflections of his character; they are not the equivalent of tape-recordings of his words, sten-
ographic reports of his utterances, or cinematographic reproduc-
tions of his deeds.

e. Though twentieth century readers of the gospels often seek
to psychoanalyze the historical Jesus or to speculate about his consciousness on the basis of these accounts, they are often unaware of
the problems inherent in such speculation. It would be easier to
psychoanalyze Paul of Tarsus than Jesus of Nazareth, since we have
at least a few authentic letters which come from him in which certain aspects of his character shine through. But the only thing that
we are told that Jesus wrote, he wrote "with his finger on the
ground," probably on sand (Jn 8:6, 8), and the evangelist did not
bother to record what it was! The one statement written about him
during his lifetime, the "title" on the cross, appears with *different*
wording in each gospel (see Mk 15:26; Mt 27:37; Lk 23:38;
Jn 19:19).

f. Modern interpreters of the gospels, however, generally acknowledge that there is a group of scenes in the ministry, a group of
sayings (mainly isolated logia and parables), and the nucleus of the
passion story that would have to be regarded as historical. But each
passage preserving these details would have to be scrutinized and
examined for its possibly editorial embellishments. Negative criteria
for Jesus' teaching have been widely accepted: Whatever does not
stem clearly from the Old Testament or contemporary Jewish teaching or does not betray the concerns of (later) early-church contro-

versy, debate, or casuistry should be ascribed to him. Other criteria,
less widely admitted, for judging his teaching have also been invoked: the principle of multiple, independent attestation (e.g. the
Pauline and synoptic tradition about Jesus' teaching on divorce);
the nuance of his eschatologically-based demand for repentance.
These criteria tend to give us a *minimum* of his teaching, what is
necessarily historical. But even they are not the final word of decision. For they are open to the obvious objection that one cannot rule
out that Jesus actually taught what other Jewish teachers might have
taught or what the Old Testament teaches. However, they do represent the earnest attempt of modern scholars to cope with the problem that the words and teaching of Jesus in the gospels present.

g. A brief sketch of what is known of the historical Jesus might
run somewhat like this. He was a Palestinian Jew, born of a woman
named Mary married to a carpenter, Joseph. He lived in Nazareth of
Galilee, having been born in the last days of Herod the Great (37–4
B.C.). He began a ministry of preaching and teaching about the
fifteenth year of Tiberius (A.D. 28), the date given for the ministry
of John the Baptist (Lk 3:1), to which his own ministry was related.
Jesus' ministry was centered in Capernaum in Galilee, at least at the
outset, though it was not confined there. He preached in Galilee in
the tetrarchy of Herod Antipas, who had imprisoned and executed
John, during the prefecture of Pontius Pilate (A.D. 23–36) and high
priesthood of Caiaphas (A.D. 18–36). The length of his ministry
cannot be established with certainty, possibly a minimum of three
years (determined by possible allusions to three Passovers in Jn
2:13, 23; 6:4[?]; 11:55, but the Johannine references are scarcely
meant as a complete list, and the synoptics know of only one
Passover).

As a Palestinian religious teacher, he came under the influence
of contemporary Jewish religious, ethical, and apocalyptic thinking;
at times he disagreed with other Jewish teachers (in his attitude

toward the temple, the Mosaic law, the observance of the sabbath, and other traditions of the fathers; see §10–11 below for some more specific themes of his preaching and teaching). His differences with other Jewish teachers manifested itself in particularly acute fashion with Pharisees, Sadducees, and others who professed to be interpreters of the Hebrew scriptures for the people. He gathered about him a group of disciples or followers, prominent among whom were Simon bar Jonah (or John) and his brother Andrew, and two of the sons of Zebedee, John and James. Twelve of these disciples he associated closely with himself and his work, but their relationship to the rest of his followers during his ministry cannot be further determined. It is not easy to say whether or not he set down a definite way of life for them. The obvious horror repeatedly associated with the name of Judas Iscariot in New Testament recollections, "one of the twelve" (Mk 14:10, 20, 43; Jn 6:70–71; cf. Mk 3:14, 19; Mt 10:2, 4; Lk 6:13, 16), eloquently testifies to the formation of the twelve as a choice of Jesus himself in his ministry.

That ministry eventually brought him to Jerusalem, and on one occasion, about the time of Passover, he was arrested with the connivance of Judas Iscariot. Interrogated by leaders of the Jewish people in Jerusalem and brought by them before Pontius Pilate, the Roman prefect of Judea, he was condemned to death and crucified outside the city and buried the same day.

Days later, on the first day of the week, his tomb was found empty, and his followers soon reported appearances of him alive, as "raised" from the dead (1 Cor 15:4). A twofold list of witnesses of the risen Christ is preserved in 1 Corinthians 15:5–7: (a) Cephas (the official first witness—see Lk 24:34), the twelve, more than five hundred disciples; (b) James, and all the apostles.

h. To the ministry and activity of the historical Jesus the earliest New Testament writer, Paul of Tarsus, traces his "gospel," his call (Gal 1:12, 16) to be an "apostle to the Gentiles" (Rom 11:13), and, by implication, his insight into Christians as the "body of Christ" (1 Cor 12:27–28). But the Jesus of history had already become for Paul "Jesus our Lord" (1 Cor 9:1).

3. Do the Apocryphal Gospels Tell Us Anything Important About Jesus of Nazareth?

The apocryphal gospels occasionally preserve some primitive tradition about Jesus, but by and large they are merely imaginative outgrowths of the canonical gospel tradition.

a. "Apocrypha," in a generic sense, are writings that grew out of the canonical Old and New Testaments. The name means "hidden," and it was used in antiquity to designate those writings related to the two Testaments that were not considered to be scripture either for Jews or for Christians. They were "hidden" from use and were not considered authoritative or canonical. They are a form of *para-biblical* literature, having grown up *alongside* of the biblical books or emerged from them. In a specific sense, "apocrypha" is the name used by Christians of the Protestant tradition for seven books of the Old Testament, which Roman Catholics often call "deuterocanonical," i.e. canonical, but in a secondary sense, since most of them (apart from Sirach) are preserved only in Greek. But there are also other apocryphal Old Testament writings (such as *1 Enoch, Jubilees, Testaments of the Twelve Patriarchs*), which develop ideas or themes in the canonical Old Testament writings. Similarly, there are apocryphal gospels, apocryphal acts, apocryphal epistles, and apocryphal apocalypses, writings that are imitative of and related to the New Testament.

b. The apocryphal gospels are, by and large, an outgrowth of the gospel tradition, which was rooted in the ministry and life of Jesus of Nazareth. That tradition developed in phases, somewhat along these lines: (1) it began with the kerygma, the primitive Christian proclamation of the Christ-event—something like 1 Corinthians 15:3–5 or Acts 2:36 ("This Jesus whom you crucified God has raised up and made Lord and messiah"); then (2) there developed *a primitive passion narrative,* something like Mark 14:1–16:8; then (3) *a primitive gospel,* a passion narrative preceded by a ministry narrative beginning with the baptism of John the Baptist, something like Mark 1:1–16:8; then (4) *a fuller gospel,* which built on Mark 1:1–16:8 and added an infancy narrative or a preliminary prologue, something like canonical Matthew or Luke, and independently of them, but parallel to them, the Johannine gospel; and finally (5) *the apocryphal gospels,* which imitated the canonical four, filling in details about Jesus' life and ministry, authentic details that may have been derived from an early oral tradition, but mainly imaginative details that sought to fill in the lacunae of the canonical gospels.

   c. Among the apocryphal gospels are such writings as:

     (1) *Gospel according to Thomas,* to which we have already referred in §2b. (See *NHLE,* 124–38.)

     (2) *Protevangelium Jacobi,* or proto-gospel of James, dating from the end of the second century. It fills in details that may come from a primitive, authentic tradition, but more likely supplies such details from imaginative speculation. In this work we learn about the life of Mary, the mother of Jesus, the names of her parents (Ann and Joachim), her presentation in the temple, her marriage to Joseph, her elderly husband who already had children by an earlier marriage, etc. (See *HSNTA,* 1. 371–88.)

     (3) *Gospel of Peter,* dating from about A.D. 150 and coming undoubtedly from Syria. It fills in details about the trial, death, and resurrection of Jesus. (See *HSNTA,* 1. 179–87; and §18 below.)

     (4) *Gospel of Truth,* a gnostic gospel, related to the school of Valentinus, and composed ca. A.D. 140–180. It is a homily that meditates on the salvific work of Jesus Christ and stresses that knowledge of the Father destroys all ignorance, the human condition in this earthly life. It contains

no narrative of the ministry, deeds, teaching, death, or resurrection of Jesus. (See *NHLE,* 38–51.)

(5) *Gospel of Thomas the Contender,* dating from the first half of the third century A.D. and coming from Edessa in Syria. It is not a gospel in the canonical sense, but a dialogue between the risen Christ and Jude Thomas, who is called in it the "twin and true companion" of Jesus. It purports to disclose "secret sayings" of the savior, but is a typical revelation dialogue. (See *NHLE,* 199–207.)

(6) *Gospel of Philip,* dating from the second half of the third century A.D. and coming probably from Syria. It has no narrative of Jesus' life or ministry, but recounts a few deeds or words of Jesus (seventeen sayings, nine of which are parallel to sayings in the canonical gospels). It compiles statements about the meaning and value of sacraments in the Valentinan gnostic system: the mysteries of the bridal chamber, distinguishing those who may enter it (free men and virgins) from those who may not (animals, slaves, defiled women). (See *NHLE,* 139–60.)

(7) *Infancy Gospel of Thomas the Philosopher of Israel,* dating from the end of the second century A.D. and written by a Gentile Christian. It narrates the miraculous deeds of the child Jesus between the age of five and twelve (e.g. his profaning of the sabbath by fashioning clay sparrows, which come to life and fly away as he claps his hands at them and says, "Off with you!"). It ends with the Lucan story of his visit as a twelve year old to Jerusalem. (See *HSNTA,* 1. 388–401.)

(8) *Gospel of the Egyptians I,* dating probably from the third century A.D. It is known only from fragments in the *Stromateis* of Clement of Alexandria and the *Panarion* of Epiphanius. It seems to have been Encratite in origin and

discusses marriage and the begetting of children. (See
HSNTA, 1. 166–78.)

(9) *Gospel of the Egyptians II,* dating probably from the third
century A.D. It is a Coptic gnostic gospel that propounds
Sethian gnostic mythology. Seth is portrayed as the father
of the gnostics, and it describes his life and his work of
salvation (especially through baptism). (See *NHLE,*
208–19.)

(10) Other fragmentary apocryphal gospels could also be mentioned, such as the *Gospel of Mary* [Magdalene] (*NHLE,*
523–27), the *Gospel of the Nazaraeans* (*HSNTA,* 1. 139–
53), the *Gospel of the Ebionites* (*HSNTA,* 1. 153–58), the
Gospel of the Hebrews (*HSNTA,* 1. 158–65), and the *Gospel of the Twelve* (*HSNTA,* 1. 263–71).

d. Despite the contentions of some modern scholars (H. Koes-
ter, J.D. Crossan), these apocryphal gospels are scarcely a source of
real information about Jesus of Nazareth. Details in them, however,
have to be scrutinized, and some of them may preserve information
that is authentic.

**4.   Is Not Such an Approach to the Jesus of History and
to the Canonical Gospels Tantamount to an Implicit Reduction
in Christian Faith and Contrary to a Centuries-Long Tradition
of Gospel Interpretation?**

At first sight, it may seem so, but in the long run such an approach is the end-product of a mode of interpretation within the
Christian community and the Roman Catholic Church that has
been a-brewing since the renaissance at least, when the first critical
studies of the gospels and of the New Testament began.

a. At first these studies concerned the text of the Greek New

Testament, when the thrust of scholarly interest within the Christian community centered on a return *ad fontes* ("back to the sources"). The debate then involved the esteem to be accorded to the ancient Greek manuscripts of the New Testament, which were gradually coming to light, over against the Latin Vulgate, which had been used for so long in the western church. Then, too, it also concerned the better Greek manuscripts over against the *Textus Receptus* or what we now call the (inferior) Byzantine or Koine text-tradition. Today, when our critical Greek New Testament texts are based on the best ancient Greek manuscripts, we realize how primitive the critical discussion of the Greek New Testament text was at that time.

b. Later the critical discussion concerned the nature of the Greek language in which the New Testament was written. Since it was clearly different from (some even said "inferior to") classical Greek, was it the language of the Holy Spirit, inspired and shaped for the transmission of the Christian "word of God," or was it simply written in a form of Hellenistic Greek, such as was being gradually made known by the discovery of Greek papyrus texts in Egypt?

c. At the end of the eighteenth century, the critical interpretation of the gospels moved to source criticism, the analysis of the relationship among the synoptic gospels, one to the other (see §1d above for the various theories eventually proposed). For it became clear that the synoptics were not independent distillations of a previous oral tradition, as was often thought.

d. At the beginning of the twentieth century, this source criticism, which had reached an impasse, gave way to form criticism, in which the units of the synoptic tradition were studied to ascertain their (stylized) form and the history of their transmission from one gospel to another. From this study emerged the form-critical categories: the sayings and parables of Jesus, the miracle-stories, the pronouncement-stories (narratives preserved because of the pronouncement or "punch line" enshrined in them [see further §12 below]), and finally stories about Jesus, John the Baptist, or the disciples (the narrative tradition proper).

e. Form criticism, which tended to be atomistic and to say little about the gospels as a whole and as we have them, gave rise to two other forms of interpretation, redaction criticism and composition criticism. Both sought to study the gospel as a whole, but the former investigated how the evangelist had shaped and modified the material that he had inherited for his own literary and theological purposes. The latter studied how the evangelist freely composed material to improve his narrative account or collection of Jesus' sayings.

f. While these kinds of criticism (source, form, redaction, and composition criticism) were being used in the interpretation of the gospels, there were also at work modern forms of literary criticism which sought to analyze poetic, rhetorical, symbolical, dramatic, and narrative techniques used by the evangelists. Thus many modern tools of historical and literary interpretation came to be used in the study of the gospels as in other types of literature, especially of ancient classical (Latin and Greek) literature.

g. This sophisticated mode of gospel interpretation was unknown in earlier centuries of the church, even though primitive elements of it did manifest themselves in the interpretation of patristic writers such as Origen, Jerome, and Augustine. It was born of the mode of studying literature inherited by twentieth century readers from the renaissance and enlightenment. Today it is no little affected by the mentality formed by contemporary news media (especially that of the *New York Times* or *The Times* of London).

It is not that twentieth century interpreters arrogantly maintain that they now have a key to the scriptures that was lacking in former centuries. They are, however, aware that the archaeological and papyrological discoveries of the late eighteenth and nineteenth centuries have opened up bodies of literature from ancient Mesopotamia, Canaan, Egypt, Asia Minor, and Palestine which Christians of

former generations and centuries never knew. The study of the ancient texts of the Bible cannot be isolated, one now realizes, from
comparable literary forms and narratives that such discoveries have
brought to light, only in recent centuries in God's providence. One
realizes today that the Bible is not one book, but a complex of diver-
sified books, the result of a long process of growth, made up of
writings comparable to literary texts of diverse ages and traditions,
and that it cannot be interpreted in isolation, as if it dropped from
heaven in King James English!

   h. The major result of such critical study of the gospels has
been the realization that the gospel tradition enshrines within it
three sorts of material about Jesus of Nazareth. These are the three
stages of the gospel tradition with which any proper reading and
study of the gospels must cope.

   First, that tradition is rooted in *what Jesus of Nazareth did and
said* during the course of his earthly ministry in Galilee and Judea
and their environs (Stage I). This would represent the stage of his
ipsissima verba (his "very words"), including the modes that he
chose to express his preaching and teaching about God, the kingdom, and himself. These were the words and deeds of a Galilean Jew
who lived roughly from A.D. 1 to 33 (to use traditional dates): his
encounters, his actions, his mode of speech (usually in Aramaic)
would have been those of a Galilean Jew of that time.

   Second, that tradition built upon *what the apostles and disciples preached about Jesus* after his death, from roughly A.D. 33 to
65 (Stage II). At this stage Jesus the preacher had become the
preached one, and the testimony borne to him and his mission had
been suffused with faith in him as the risen Lord and Christ (Acts
2:36). The faithful explanation of his deeds and words passed on by
the apostles and disciples was reproduced with what is often called
"Easter-faith," i.e. with an added understanding and a new comprehension of him, his words, his deeds, and his impact as a whole, even

his divinity. This came only with their faith in him and experience of him as the risen and glorified Lord: "His disciples did not understand this at first; but when Jesus was glorified, then they remembered that what had been written of him was what they had done to him" (Jn 12:16; cf. 2:22). Yet none of these disciple-preachers ever sought to reproduce with factual accuracy the words and deeds of Jesus himself; they understood those words and deeds with hindsight and adapted them to the needs of those to whom they preached.

Third, that tradition developed into *what the evangelists wrote down about him* in their various gospels, between A.D. 65 and 95 (Stage III). Part of the tradition of Stage II may already have existed in writing before the evangelists composed their gospels, e.g. the Greek "Q" material, which is postulated to have been in written form before the Lucan and Matthean gospels, but which has not been preserved as such. Pursuing a method and a goal peculiar to each one, the evangelists used the tradition that had grown up about him in the preaching of Stage II: they *selected* material from it (sayings and parables, miracle stories, pronouncement stories, and stories about him, about John the Baptist, and about the apostles), *synthesized* it into their own literary compositions, *explicated* it, as needed, by redactional modifications and additions, and *fashioned* it all into a unique literary form that we call "gospel," indeed, into the four accounts known as the canonical gospels. This means, then, that none of the evangelists was an eyewitness of Jesus' ministry. They heard about Jesus and his ministry from others who were "eyewitnesses" and who had become "ministers of the word" (Lk 1:2). The result is that the evangelists picked up traditional material and fashioned it into their accounts as they saw fit, and not necessarily with factual accuracy. For instance, the account of the purging of the Jerusalem temple by Jesus occurs at the beginning of his ministry in John's gospel (2:13–16), but in the synoptics at the time of

Jesus' visit to Jerusalem shortly before his death (Mk 11:15–17; Mt 21:12–13; Lk 19:45–46). That also means that none of the evangelists has recorded Jesus' words and deeds simply for the sake of *remembering* them. What the early tradition "remembered" about his ministry has been made to serve the purpose of the gospel accounts, to stir up faith in him.

Still other material from Stage II, the transmission of which did not cease to grow with the composition of the canonical gospels, resulted in other gospel forms that the later Christian community eventually did not consider as authentic or "recognized" (*homologoumena,* to use Eusebius' term for the canonical writings, *Hist. eccl.* 3.25,3). These are the so-called apocryphal gospels. By and large they scarcely reflect Stage I (see §2b and 3 above).

This threefold distinction of the gospel tradition about Jesus of Nazareth is widely admitted today by interpreters in the Christian tradition of various confessional backgrounds, even though all may not use the same terminology for it.

i. In the Roman Catholic communion this mode of interpretation of the gospels and this distinction of stages of the gospel tradition have found modern support in three ecclesiastical documents of this century: (1) *Divino afflante Spiritu.* Pope Pius XII's encyclical of 1943 on the promotion of biblical studies strongly insisted on the study of literary forms in the Bible as the key to the interpretation of it (§35–39; *AAS* 35 [1943] 314–17; *EnchBib* §558–60; *RSS* 97–99). This insistence gave implicit encouragement to the use of form criticism by Roman Catholic interpreters, even in the study of the gospels. (2) *Instructio de historica evangeliorum veritate.* The "Instruction on the Historical Truth of the Gospels" of the Biblical Commission in 1964 espoused explicitly the form-critical and redaction-critical methods of interpretation of the gospels and made use of the three stages of the tradition mentioned above (see further the Appendix). (3) *Dei Verbum,* §19. The Dogmatic Constitution on

Divine Revelation of Vatican Council II (1965) succinctly recapitulated in one brief paragraph the teaching of the Biblical Commission's Instruction, thus making it its own view of gospel interpretation (see the Appendix). Thus such interpretation of the gospels has the support not only of a Vatican commission, but even of the council fathers. Hence even church authorities have today espoused the modern critical interpretation of the canonical gospels, recognizing that in God's providence a key to the interpretation of them has indeed been given to the Christian community which it did not have in earlier centuries, which has opened up in a remarkable, undreamed-of way the treasures of these biblical writings, and which is *neglected only to the detriment of Christian faith itself.*

Why in this age? An easy answer is to refer to the great ecumenical advances between Roman Catholics and other Christians born of the reformation. The rapprochement that has taken place between these two historic Christian groups in the interpretation of the Bible can only be explained by the adoption of this mode of historical-critical interpretation of scripture unknown earlier.

j. Finally, it should be apparent that the error in any simplistic or fundamentalist approach to the gospels is precisely the confusing of Stage III with Stage I of the gospel tradition. At least a generation elapsed between them, during which what was remembered about Jesus of Stage I was subject to much constructive Christian reflection born of faith in him as Christ the Lord. What the evangelists have put on the lips of Jesus is not simply his "very words" (*ipsissima verba*), without further ado. It may well rest on something that he had said, but that "something" has to be ferreted out in each instance with form-critical and redaction-critical methods. What the gospels present to us from Stage I has been filtered through the tradition of Stage II and the selective, editorial, and explicative process of Stage III. In other words, the gospels show us how Jesus was presented to Christian readers about A.D. 65 (Mark), or about A.D.

80 (Matthew, Luke), or about A.D. 90 (John). Indirectly they also supply us with evidence of how Jesus was preached as "Lord and Messiah" during the 30s, 40s, and 50s, and in that preaching how he was perceived to have been in his ministry ca. A.D. 30.

To pretend that Stage III equals Stage I is a form of naiveté. It can have disastrous effects eventually, as has often been attested: either intellectual suicide (a refusal to think and use one's intellect, God's greatest natural gift to human beings) or a total loss of faith (a failure to follow where his Spirit guides the Christian community).

5. How Historical Are the Infancy Narratives of the Matthean and Lucan Gospels?

The infancy narratives have an historical nucleus, but apart from that it is difficult to say how much else in them is to be considered historical.

a. The infancy narratives do not stem from the earliest stage of the gospel tradition. The Marcan gospel lacks such a narrative, and the Johannine gospel, which is recognized to be a product of an equally early tradition that grew up in independence of the synoptics, likewise lacks such a narrative. It has instead the prologue about the Word made flesh (1:1–18). The infancy narratives emerged at a point in the tradition when people in the early church began to ask about Jesus' background and his forebears. Thus these narratives corresponded to a biographical interest that eventually surfaced in the gospel tradition. They reply to such questions as *Quis? et Unde?:* "Who is he? and Where did he come from?" The narratives have been prefixed in the gospel tradition to the part that otherwise began with the account of the appearance of John the Baptist as the preacher of baptism and repentance, Matthew 3:1–3 and Luke 3:2–4, which corresponds to the beginning of the Marcan gospel (1:2–4). The appearance of John the Baptist is likewise the beginning of the tradition enshrined in the Johannine gospel (in the prose inserts in the prologue [1:6–7, 15] and in the sequel to the prologue [1:19–27]).

b. The Matthean infancy narrative differs considerably from the Lucan. The Matthean narrative has six episodes: the genealogy of Jesus (1:1–17), in descending order from Abraham to Joseph; and five episodes that climax in or end with an Old Testament quotation: the account of the virginal conception of Jesus (1:18–25); the visit of the magi (2:1–12); the flight to Egypt (2:13–15); the massacre of the innocents (2:16–18); and the return from Egypt to Nazareth (2:19–23). The Lucan infancy narrative, however, has nothing corresponding to Matthew 2:1–23, and its structure is quite different, being built principally on a parallelism of the announcements of the conception of John the Baptist (1:5–23) and Jesus (1:26–38), of the births of John (1:57–58) and Jesus (2:1–4), of the circumcision and manifestation of John (1:59–80) and Jesus (2:21), with intervening episodes. Again, the Matthean infancy narrative has nothing about John the Baptist or what would correspond to Luke 2:8–52 (the coming of the shepherds to Bethlehem, the presentation of Jesus in the temple, the visit of the twelve year old Jesus to the temple). Moreover, in the Matthean narrative Joseph receives the heavenly communication about Mary's virginal conception (1:20–21, from the angel of the Lord [unnamed] in a dream), whereas in the Lucan narrative Mary receives it (1:28–35, from Gabriel). If we had only the Lucan narrative, we would conclude that Jesus must have known John, his kinsman (born of Elizabeth, the kinswoman of Mary, 1:36). Yet in John's gospel the Baptist declares, "I myself did not know him" (1:31), a peculiar admission if Luke's infancy narrative is accurate in this regard. Such differences make it difficult to harmonize the details of the Matthean and Lucan infancy narratives and to square some of the details with other inherited gospel traditions. All of this has a bearing on the question whether all the details in the infancy narratives are recounted as historically factual.

c. Most New Testament interpreters, in analyzing the relationship of the synoptic gospels, admit that Matthew and Luke used

Mark and "Q," but insist that neither Matthew depended on Luke, nor Luke on Matthew (see §1d above). Given such a solution to the synoptic problem, the Lucan infancy narrative evidently does not depend on the Matthean, or vice versa. This, then, accounts for the diversity in the two infancy narratives and shows that each evangelist, in constructing his infancy narrative, did so independently and for distinct literary purposes (Matthew, to stress the fulfillment of Old Testament motifs; Luke, to emphasize the parallelism of God's intervention in the conception and birth of John and Jesus).

d. Despite such independence and differences, however, there are twelve points in which Matthew and Luke agree in their infancy narratives:

(1) Jesus' birth is related to the reign of Herod the Great (Mt 2:1; Lk 1:5).

(2) Mary, his mother to be, is a virgin engaged to Joseph, but they have not yet come to live together (Mt 1:18; Lk 1:27, 34; 2:5).

(3) Joseph is of the house of David (Mt 1:16, 20; Lk 1:27; 2:4).

(4) An angel from heaven announces the coming conception and birth of Jesus (Mt 1:20–21; Lk 1:28–30).

(5) Jesus himself is recognized to be a son of David (Mt 1:1; Lk 1:32).

(6) His conception is to take place through the Holy Spirit (Mt 1:18, 20; Lk 1:35).

(7) Joseph is not involved in the conception (Mt 1:18–25; Lk 1:34).

(8) The name "Jesus" is imposed by heaven prior to his birth (Mt 1:21; Lk 1:31).

(9) Heaven identifies Jesus as "Savior" (Mt 1:21; Lk 2:11).

(10) Jesus is born after Joseph and Mary come to live together (Mt 1:24–25; Lk 2:4–7).

(11) Jesus is born at Bethlehem (Mt 2:1; Lk 2:4–7).

(12) Jesus settles, with Mary and Joseph, in Nazareth in Galilee (Mt 2:22–23; Lk 2:39, 51).

In these twelve points one can use Matthew as a check or an historical control on Luke and vice versa, since this is an instance of multiple, independent attestation. Both Matthew and Luke have inherited common earlier traditions about the infancy of Jesus. Each of them has adopted such details, which may be regarded as the historical nucleus, and incorporated them into his own structured literary composition.

As for the other details in the two infancy narratives, beyond these twelve that have been inherited in common, they may have come from the private sources that both Matthew and Luke have used, from "M" or "L." But no one can be sure about the use of "M" and "L" in this part of the gospel tradition; one cannot exclude the likelihood that both Matthew and Luke have freely composed their narratives, while making use of these twelve points. If so, then one has to allow for doubts and hesitation about the historical character of the rest (e.g. in the Matthean narrative, about the visit of the magi, the flight to Egypt, the massacre of the innocents, the return to Nazareth; similarly in the Lucan narrative, the visit of the shepherds, the presentation in the temple, the finding of the twelve year old Jesus in the temple). Such details have no counterpart in the other infancy narrative, and there is nothing like an historical control for them. Yet the historical kernel (the twelve points) prevents one from writing off the infancy narratives as mere fabrications out of whole cloth.

e. What has to be emphasized is that, even though various scenes in the Lucan and Matthean infancy narratives lack probative historical elements, they have not been incorporated into the gospels merely as *historical accounts*. Each episode in these narratives conveys its own theological and christological meaning and enhances the gospel message about the newborn Jesus, who is "the savior, Christ the Lord" (Lk 2:11). Such a meaning and message come through, even if one cannot show the historical basis of all the details in these infancy narratives.

6. Does the Story of the Virgin Birth Record Simple Historical Fact or Are There Other Possible Ways of Understanding It?

At the outset, for the sake of clarity in a discussion of New Testament data, it would be better to speak of the virginal *conception* of Jesus, because that is the only question at issue in the infancy narratives. We are concerned with what has been called Mary's *virginitas ante partum,* "virginity before the birth" (of Jesus). Nothing is said in the New Testament about the mode of Mary's giving birth to Jesus, i.e. about what later came to be called *virginitas in partu,* "virginity in the (actual) birth," i.e. without pain and without damage to her physical organs. The expression "virgin birth" has come into modern parlance because of the way in which the creeds of the early church formulated their affirmation, "born of the Holy Spirit from the Virgin Mary" ("natus est de Spiritu Sancto ex Maria virgine"; *ton gennēthenta ek pneumatos hagiou kai Marias tēs parthenou*).

a. The virginal conception of Jesus is never referred to by Paul, Mark, or the Johannine tradition; among New Testament writers the only ones who touch upon it are Matthew and Luke, and their infancy narratives date from about A.D. 80–85. Paul knows of Jesus' Davidic descent (Rom 1:3) and stresses Jesus' birth "from a woman" (Gal 4:4) in a fundamentally soteriological statement. He knows of Jesus' divine sonship and implies his pre-existence; neither of these details is considered by him to be in conflict with the two preceding facts.

Mark has no infancy narrative, and there is not the slightest trace of a belief in the virginal conception in his gospel. Because it is usually thought that the infancy narratives were the last part of the canonical gospel tradition to take shape, the narrative about the virginal conception in the Matthean and Lucan gospels represents almost certainly a post-Marcan development.

Even though the Johannine gospel is the latest in its final redaction among the canonical gospels (ca. A.D. 90–95), its tradition in part goes back to a period as early as that of the earliest synoptic (Mark). But, significantly, it shows no knowledge of the developed conception-christology that manifests itself in the infancy narratives of Matthew and Luke. (The reader should not be misled by the reading of John 1:13 in *The Jerusalem Bible,* which follows a patristic tradition in reading the singular relative pronoun: "who was born not out of human stock or urge of the flesh or will of man, but of God himself." This reading suggests the virginal conception, but it is not supported by any Greek manuscript of the fourth gospel or found in any modern critical text of the Greek New Testament. *The New Jerusalem Bible* has corrected the translation of 1:13, and even admits that the singular would refer to "Jesus' divine origin, not to the virgin birth.")

b. The virginal conception of Jesus is recounted in the Matthean and Lucan infancy narratives. It is clearly asserted in Matthew 1:18–25 and, perhaps less clearly, in Luke 1:31–35. In both the Matthean and Lucan infancy narratives the evangelist intends to tell us who Jesus is and whence he comes. Through the genealogy and the angel's message to Joseph, Matthew gets across Jesus' Davidic descent and the Spirit's role in his conception; Luke presents the same two ideas, both of them in the message of Gabriel to Mary. In both of these episodes we may detect a dramatization and Christian development of a christological affirmation that was once stated merely in a parallelism in the kerygmatic fragment embedded in Romans 1:3–4: "descended from David according to the flesh and constituted Son of God in power according to a spirit of holiness as of (his) resurrection from the dead." What was kerygmatically proclaimed about Jesus' relation to David and to the Spirit *as of the resurrection* was in time pressed back to his very conception in the tradition that both Matthew and Luke inherited from the Christian community. The Marcan gospel, which lacks an infancy narrative,

used the baptism scene (1:10–11) to express a similar relationship of
Jesus to God involving the Spirit. This relationship constitutes the
major doctrinal affirmation of the Matthean and Lucan stories of
the virginal conception of Jesus; their main thrust is an affirmation
about Jesus, not about Mary ever-Virgin.

c. Neither the Lucan nor the Matthean infancy narrative reckons with the pre-existence or the incarnation of Christ. These elements of a "high" (or highly developed) christology may have been
at home in an earlier stage of the New Testament tradition (e.g. see
Phil 2:6–11 and the comments made in §17b). But the christology of
the infancy narratives is "higher" than that of the Marcan gospel in
presenting Jesus' relation to God through the Spirit as something
now realized to be true as of his very conception.

d. What we have said so far sums up the matter of Jesus' conception in terms of christological assertion, or, as some prefer to call
it, as a theologoumenon, or possibly as a *Glaubensaussage,* an "affirmation of faith." That it certainly is. It is possible to understand
the virginal conception of Jesus, as described in the New Testament,
solely in this way (recall the wording of the question). But is the
account of the virginal conception also intended as an affirmation of
"historical fact"? It has, indeed, been so understood by New Testament interpreters (e.g. H. Schürmann, who would trace it to an
"intimate family tradition"); it has been understood as historical
and based in part on public knowledge of Mary's early pregnancy
before she came to live with Joseph (see Mt 1:18c). But how would
the public have come to know of it "as of the Holy Spirit"? Or, if
Mary knew from the beginning that Jesus had no human father,
why was there only such a gradual development in christology? It is
hard to explain, however, how such a tradition would have developed if it were not based on fact. Yet in this matter, which needs far
more discussion than space permits here, one can only say, with
R.E. Brown, that "the *scientifically controllable* biblical evidence

leaves [the question of the historicity of the virginal conception] an unresolved problem" (*The Virginal Conception and Bodily Resurrection of Jesus* [New York/Paramus, NJ: Paulist, 1973] 66). But Brown also acknowledges that for Roman Catholics the long-standing church tradition about Mary's perpetual virginity supplies an answer to that part of the question.

e. It is good to recall that even in the gospels, which have an infancy narrative and assert the virginal conception of Jesus, there are elements of a tradition which either do not reckon with it or have not been integrated into such a belief. For instance, Luke 2:41 speaks of Mary and Joseph as "his parents" (cf. v. 43), and Mary says to the twelve year old Jesus, "Your father and I have been looking for you" (2:48). This is simply said, with no qualification such as "foster father" or "putative father." And Matthew 13:55 records the query, "Is not this the carpenter's son?" Again, the genealogies trace Jesus' pedigree through Joseph (Mt 1:16; Lk 3:23 [with the corrective, "as was supposed," which does integrate the Lucan genealogy into the belief about the virginal conception]). Cf. Jn 6:42.

f. In sum, one has to recognize that the New Testament data about this question are not unambiguous; they do not necessarily support the claim that this belief was a matter of "the constant teaching of the Church from the beginning" (M. Schmaus, "Mariology," *Sacramentum mundi* [New York: Herder and Herder, 1968–70], 3.379). The data suggest rather that this belief became part of the developing christology of the early church, within New Testament times, to be sure, but they are not part of the *earliest* tradition.

In this matter one should consult R.E. Brown, *The Birth of the Messiah* (Garden City, NY: Doubleday, 1977) 517–33; R.E. Brown et al. (eds.), *Mary in the New Testament: A Collaborative Assessment by Protestant and Roman Catholic Scholars* (New York: Paulist; Philadelphia: Fortress, 1978) 74–134; and my article, "The Virginal Conception of Jesus in the New Testament," *TS* 34 (1973) 541–75, now reprinted with a postscript in *To Advance the Gospel: New Testament Studies* (New York: Crossroad, 1981) 41–78.

7. How Are We To Understand the References to the Brothers and Sisters of Jesus in the New Testament?

The main references to Jesus' brothers and sisters in the New Testament are found in the episode of Jesus' visit to "his own country" (Mk 6:1–3): "Is not this the carpenter, the son of Mary and brother of James and Joses and Judas and Simon, and are not his sisters here with us?" Cf. Mt 13:55–56, which has a slightly different formulation. See also Mk 3:32; Mt 12:46. The Johannine tradition mentions "his mother and brothers" (2:12), but also records that "his brothers" did not believe in him (7:5). Likewise, Paul knows of James of Jerusalem as a "brother of the Lord" (Gal 1:19; recall Josephus' echo of this tradition, quoted in §2a above). Do these references mean "blood brothers and sisters, siblings" or are they to be understood otherwise?

a. Some interpreters, recalling the long tradition about Mary as *aeiparthenos* or "semper virgo" (DS 44, 46), prefer to understand the phrases in a broader sense. Many Protestant interpreters, however, understand them to mean blood brothers or sisters, siblings. The perpetual virginity of Mary is well attested in the third century, and by implication is already found in the second century writing, *Protevangelium Jacobi* (*HSNTA*, 1. 374–88, esp. 9:2; 17:1; 18:1 [children of Joseph from a former marriage]; see *Mary in the New Testament*, 273–75). But the question is complicated by the New Testament evidence itself; the answer rests not on the later ecclesiastical tradition alone.

b. Matthew 1:25 has to be interpreted carefully: "He [Joseph] knew her not until (*heōs [hou]*) she had borne a son." This has often been thought to mean that Mary's virginity was preserved until the

birth of Jesus (*virginitas ante partum*), but that after it Joseph had
intercourse with her. A careful analysis of the passage (vv. 18–25),
however, reveals that Matthew's primary intention was to assert
lack of intercourse in the time that preceded the birth of Jesus and in
relation to Isaiah 7:14 (LXX: a virgin who conceives and bears a
son). Verse 25, then, asserts that Mary remained a virgin even until
Jesus was born. It says nothing about any marital relations after the
birth of Jesus. It is only when Matthew 1:25 is read in conjunction
with Mark 6:1–3 or Matthew 13:55–56 that one begins to ask
whether something more may be implied there. Per se, however,
Matthew 1:25 does not imply *virginitas post partum* (virginity after
the birth [of Jesus]), nor does it deny it. The whole issue raises a
further question about how dependent the traditions in the infancy
narrative were on the rest of the traditions of that gospel.

    c. It is well known that Greek *adelphos* may mean something
more than merely "blood brother" (e.g. "co-religionist" [Rom 9:3],
"neighbor" [Mt 5:22–24], "step-brother" [Mk 6:17–18], "kinsman,
relative" [Gen 29:12; 24:48]; in the last sense it merely reflects the
broad sense of Hebrew *'āh* or Aramaic *'ăhā'*). The question is
whether this sense of "relative, kinsman" could possibly have been
meant in the phrases of Mark 6:1–3. Is there any basis in the New
Testament for so understanding it? (N.B. The New Testament has a
word for "cousin" [Col 4:10, *anepsios*]; so this meaning should not
be foisted on *adelphos*.)

    d. Mark 15:40 supplies a reason for raising the question about
the meaning of *adelphos.* It lists three women standing at a distance
from the cross and looking at the crucified Jesus: Mary Magdalene,
Mary the mother of James the younger and of Joses, and Salome. It
is hardly likely, however, that the evangelist would be using such a
circumlocution as "Mary the mother of James the younger and of
Joses" to designate the mother of the person hanging on the cross.
He would have almost certainly said "his mother" or "the mother of
Jesus." Moreover, it is only in the Johannine tradition that it is
reported that "his mother" was standing by the cross (19:25). The

synoptic tradition knows nothing of this. But since the sons James and Joses are two of the *adelphoi* mentioned in Mark 6:3, the question is then raised: In what sense is *adelphos* used there? If it means "blood brother," then it would imply that Mark was using a strange circumlocution to say that Mary, the mother of Jesus, was standing at a distance from the cross. But if the phrase in 15:40 does not refer to the mother of the crucified Jesus, then Mark 15:40 would seem to suggest that *adelphos* in 6:3 is to be understood in a sense other than "blood brother," e.g. "relative, kinsman." See also Mk 15:47; 16:1; cf. Mt 27:56, 61; 28:1.

In other words the New Testament itself is ambiguous about the meaning of *adelphos* in Mark 6:3, when that verse is compared with Mark 15:40, 47; 16:1. This ambiguity bears, then, on the question of Mary's perpetual virginity. It means that one cannot solve easily, on the basis of the New Testament evidence alone, the question whether Jesus' "brothers and sisters" have to be understood in the strict sense of siblings or in the broad sense of kinsmen, relatives. The latter possibility is certainly not ruled out.

8. How Are the Gospel Accounts of Jesus' Baptism To Be Understood?

References to Jesus' baptism are found in all four gospels (Mk 1:9–11; Mt 3:13–17; Lk 3:21–22; Jn 1:30–34) and indirectly in Acts (10:37–38). There is no reason to question the historicity of the fact that Jesus of Nazareth, toward the beginning of his own ministry, submitted himself to a ritual washing performed by John the Baptist. The indirect reference to the baptism in the speech of Peter in Acts 10 may simply reflect Luke's own account in 3:21–22. However, some have thought that Peter's speech at the conversion of Cornelius contains a brief summary of early Christian kerygmatic preaching (see C.H. Dodd, *The Apostolic Preaching and Its Developments* [London: Hodder and Stoughton, 1936] 478). If that theory has any validity, then the reference may be even earlier than that in Mark 1:9–11 and may provide an independent early attestation to the same event.

a. John's baptizing is attested extrabiblically. Josephus (*Ant.* 18.5,2 §116–17) refers to him as one "called the Baptist," knows of his *baptismos,* and speaks of it in connection with a pardon of sins. Moreover, John's baptism can be plausibly viewed against the background of the ritual washings in the contemporary Palestinian Jewish Qumran community, which practiced (daily) lustrations in a belief that they symbolized God's refinement (by fire) of the human frame and a purification of it by "a spirit of holiness" (*Manual of Discipline* [1QS] 4:20–22). The synoptic gospels have related John's baptism to his preaching of repentance for the forgiveness of sins (Mk 1:4, 5; Mt 3:6, 11; Lk 3:3).

b. There are differences of detail in the gospel accounts of the baptism of Jesus. Whereas all four evangelists relate the incident to the River Jordan, they do so with slight differences (see Mk 1:9; Mt 3:13; Lk 3:3; 4:1; Jn 1:28; 3:26 ["beyond the Jordan"]). The differences in other details are more pronounced. In Mark 1:9 and Matthew 3:13–16, Jesus is explicitly baptized by John, whereas in Luke 3:21–22 no agent is named ("When . . . Jesus too was baptized"). The reason for Luke's silence about who baptized Jesus is that he has already recounted the imprisonment of the Baptist in vv. 19–20; he thus finishes off his story of John before he begins that of Jesus, and hence he cannot, in the logic of his own narrative sequence, mention the baptism by John. Note that in John 1:24–34 too it is never said that John baptized Jesus or even that Jesus was baptized; this is implicit, however, in the words addressed to John by him who sent him to baptize. In this difference one detects the interests of the evangelist taking precedence over mere historical detail.

In Mark 1:10, after the baptism, we are told that Jesus "saw the heavens opened and the Spirit descending on him"—an experience of Jesus himself, and no one else is said to have witnessed it. In Luke

3:21–22 Jesus, having been baptized, was at prayer, when "the heavens happened to open and the Holy Spirit descended in bodily form like a dove upon him." Here the evangelist has, as he often does elsewhere (5:16; 6:12; 9:18; 11:2; 22:32, 41; 23:46), depicted Jesus at prayer at a crucial moment of his career. But, more importantly, the opening of the heavens and the descent of the Spirit are recounted as perceptible to others. In Matthew 3:16 Jesus "saw the Spirit of God descending on him" (as in Mk 1:10), but the opening of the heavens is narrated as publicly perceptible ("Behold, the heavens were opened"). In John 1:32–33 the Baptist is the only one who saw "the Spirit descend as a dove from heaven." Hence the narratives differ as to whether Jesus or others or the Baptist perceived what was happening.

Moreover, in Mark 1:11 and Luke 3:22 the heavenly voice addresses Jesus himself, "You are my beloved Son; in you I have taken delight." But in Matthew 3:17 the heavenly voice publicly declares, "This is my beloved Son. . . ." In John 1:33 no voice from heaven is heard at the baptism or says anything about Jesus' sonship; but the one who has sent John to baptize has already told him, "As for the one on whom you see the Spirit descend and remain, he it is who baptizes with the Holy Spirit."

c. From such differences of detail it is clear that we can no longer reconstruct exactly what happened at Jesus' baptism itself (in Stage I of the gospel tradition), beyond a generic realization that early Christians associated with Jesus' baptism by John a heavenly intervention making known his elect status. But it is no longer clear how this happened or to whom the declaration was made (to Jesus? to the bystanders? to John?). This should instruct us that the importance of the scene in the gospel tradition lay in something else.

d. In the earliest gospel the baptism scene (Mk 1:9–11) serves to identify Jesus of Nazareth for the readers: he is heaven's chosen agent for the preaching of "God's gospel" (1:14), now identified as "beloved Son" (with a possible allusion to the servant-theme of Isaiah 42:1 [LXX]). This role he plays in the Marcan gospel as he subsequently is depicted preaching, teaching, healing, and announcing the kingdom of God. This initial identification of Jesus is the real import of the Marcan baptism scene, all the more important because this gospel lacks an infancy narrative and the use of christological titles associated with that part of the gospel tradition. The real question is what the baptism scene reveals to the readers of the Matthean and Lucan gospels, which have already identified Jesus with diverse titles in the infancy narratives themselves. In the case of the Lucan gospel, the infancy narrative was almost certainly prefixed at a later stage, after the composition of the bulk of the gospel. Even though Jesus has already been identified as Son of God in 1:32, 35, Luke has retained the baptism scene because it was associated with the traditional beginning of the story of Jesus' ministry and becomes important for him as the "beginning" (*archē*) of the period of Jesus in his understanding of salvation history.

e. To what extent can we determine the nature of the personal experience of the Jesus of history on the occasion of his baptism at the beginning of his public ministry? This is difficult to say. Apart from the generic problem of the consciousness of Jesus of Nazareth (see §2e above), the differences of detail in this episode compound the difficulty. Mark has clearly depicted the sequel to the baptism as a personal experience of Jesus, and Luke does so partly. But Matthew has made of the heavenly declaration a public proclamation, and John a heavenly revelation to the Baptist alone. Neither of the latter two gospels hints at what Jesus himself might have experienced.

It is often said (in popular treatments) that the baptism was the occasion when Jesus became aware that he was God's messiah. This, however, is an over-simplification. (1) The wording of the heavenly declaration in the synoptics does not identify Jesus as an anointed agent, a messiah. It speaks in terms of his sonship and possibly of his servanthood. (2) Psalm 2:7 ("You are my son; this day I have begotten you"), which is often introduced to support this interpretation, is found only in a few manuscripts, but not in the best of them, in the

Lucan tradition. Moreover, one would have to show that this royal psalm was actually understood as messianic (as referring to an *expected* messiah to sit on David's throne) in contemporary Palestinian Judaism. Yet there is no evidence to show that Palestinian Jews in pre-Christian times interpreted Psalm 2 as messianic; that idea enters Jewish thinking at a much later date. (3) Only Luke among New Testament writers interprets Jesus' baptism as his anointing with the Holy Spirit (Acts 10:38). To extrapolate from such a later Christian theological interpretation to the consciousness of Jesus of Nazareth is highly problematic.

f. A final comment has to be made about the conversation between John the Baptist and Jesus in Matthew 3:14–15 (John would have prevented Jesus from being baptized by him, saying, "I ought to be baptized by you, and are you coming to me?" Jesus answered, "Let it be so now. It is fitting for us to fulfill all righteousness in this way"). The conversation, recorded only in Matthew, gives a distinctive Matthean coloring to the baptism scene (as did the Lucan addition about Jesus at prayer); it would have to be related to the evangelist's larger theme of righteousness (cf. e.g. 21:32). Two remarks should be added: (1) The "fulfillment of all righteousness" stresses the relationship of John's ministry and baptism to God's salvific will; the Matthean Jesus, in submitting to John's baptism, acknowledges the Baptist's role and the heavenly origin of that salvific way of righteousness that John's preaching announced among his contemporaries. (2) "Let it be so now." Jesus' submission to the Baptist's washing as a sign of repentance for the remission of sins implies at least his identification of himself with sinful humanity seeking a way of righteousness given by God through John. Whether it was meant to express an awareness of sin on the part of Jesus himself is another matter. This touches again on the consciousness problem discussed above, and it may be asked whether the Matthean episode was meant to answer such a problem. John's protest reflects much more the awareness of the early church, which otherwise insisted on the sinlessness of Christ Jesus (see 2 Cor 5:21;

Jn 8:46; Heb 4:15; 7:26) and the forerunner-relation of John's baptism to early Christian baptism.

9. How Are the Gospel Accounts of Jesus' Temptations To Be Understood?

a. That Jesus of Nazareth faced temptations in his earthly life is attested in the New Testament apart from the gospel accounts. Hebrews 4:15 records that "we have not a high priest who is unable to sympathize with our weaknesses, but one who in every respect has been tempted as we are, yet without sin." Again, in Hebrews 2:18 it is said, "he himself has suffered and been tempted." Together with the gospel scenes, these verses assure the reality of temptation in the life of Jesus of Nazareth.

b. In the earliest gospel the temptation is described thus: "Immediately [after his baptism] the Spirit drove Jesus out into the desert. He was in the desert for forty days, tempted by Satan, and was with the beasts, and angels ministered to him" (Mk 1:12–13). Two brief verses thus record the event of Jesus' sojourn in the desert in the company of wild beasts as he was tempted by Satan for forty days. As in Hebrews, the mere fact is stated, and nothing is said of the nature of such temptation. As in Hebrews, where the text declares his triumph over such temptation ("yet without sin"), the Marcan text implies the same by its remark that "angels ministered to him." The Marcan scene is a sort of paradise regained.

c. In the later Matthean and Lucan parallels to the Marcan scene, the evangelists have filled in the details about the kind of temptation that Jesus underwent. Both Matthew and Luke add the "Q" account of the episode (Mt 4:3–10; Lk 4:3–12) to a form of the Marcan introduction (Mt 4:1–2; Lk 4:1–2). The order of the temptations differs. In Matthew the order is desert—pinnacle of Jerusalem temple—high mountain, whereas in Luke it is desert—high mountain (by implication)—pinnacle of Jerusalem temple. In both the Matthean and the Lucan accounts the unifying link in the three scenes is the answer given by Jesus to the tempter in a series of quotations from Deuteronomy. The original order of "Q" is undoubtedly preserved in Matthew, where Jesus replies to the tempter quoting in reverse order Deuteronomy 8:3; 6:16; 6:13, whereas the order of the last two is changed in the Lucan form to suit the evangelist's geographical perspective, his preoccupation with Jerusalem: even Jesus' last temptation takes place in the city of destiny.

d. The problem that these temptation scenes create is that they mention no witnesses of the events. They depict only Jesus and Satan. How did early Christians ever become aware of such confrontations of Jesus and this tempter? Again, apart from Matthew 4:10, where Jesus exclaims, "Begone, Satan!" all the conversation between Jesus and Satan is made up of quotations of or allusions to Old Testament passages: Satan alludes to Exodus 16 (or Numbers 11:7–8); to Deuteronomy 12:30–31 (or Exodus 23:23–33); and Exodus 17:1–7; and Jesus replies (in Matthew) by quoting Deuteronomy 8:13; 6:16; and 6:13. The upshot of this is that the "Q" temptation scenes seem to be secondary constructions. But the question is: Why would early Christians have concocted such fantastic stories about Jesus? Clearly these scenes were not meant to be understood literally (i.e. that a personal tempter confronted the Jesus of history), since at the end of the scenes, despite the transport of him to the pinnacle of the temple and to a high mountain, Jesus is still in the desert (Mt 4:11), whence he withdraws to Galilee.

A solution to the problem is found in the parabolic nature of these accounts. They are possibly to be traced back to Jesus himself, who may have recounted them to his disciples in this highly dramatic and symbolic fashion to get across to them how temptations came to him during his ministry. The opposition of his contemporaries to him and the rejection of the message that he was preaching would have been the background of the temptation to use his power to undercut such opposition and rejection. Hence he would have dramatized in such scenes that seduction to use his power to feed his

own ego apart from his Father's design, to seek notoriety and dominion from someone other than God, and to manifest himself with
éclat before his adversaries by giving them "a sign from heaven" (Mt
16:1). Thus the scenes depict him as one tempted to abandon his
role as one faithful to his Father. The message that comes through is
that he has been tested and been found faithful; he is the faithful and
obedient "Son of God." (Recall the tempter's challenge, "If you are
the Son of God . . ." [Mt 4:3, 6; Lk 4:3, 9]). Thus at the very outset of
his ministry Jesus is depicted in the Matthean and Lucan gospels not
only as heaven's "beloved Son" (at his baptism, Mt 3:17; Lk 3:22),
but also as the faithful, tested Son of God. Whether one can substan-
tiate the historicity of the temptation scenes or not, the religious
import of them is clearly delineated.

10. What Themes in the Gospels Are Accepted as Representing the Teachings of Jesus Himself?

Even though modern New Testament interpreters scrutinize
every saying or teaching put on Jesus' lips by the evangelists, there is
a general agreement about certain themes of his authentic teaching
(recall the criteria mentioned in §2f above).

One must realize at the outset that the tradition about Jesus'
ministry in both the synoptics and John transmits many teachings
about God, the kingdom, salvation, sin, ethics, and eschatology
without topical arrangement or systematic presentation. Moreover,
no synthetic body of doctrine has been ascribed to Jesus; hence
attempts to synthesize "themes" of his teaching have to be recognized for what they are, modern constructs. With this in mind, we
may single out five topics as the main themes of the preaching of the
historical Jesus.

a. The primary theme, both explicit in his sayings and parables
and implicit in his miracles and deeds, was that a new mode of
God's salvation was being offered to human beings, that Yahweh's

sovereign activity was manifesting itself anew in human history, inaugurating an era when human beings would be challenged to react in faith to this divine salvific manifestation. "Salvation" as deliverance from physical evil, personal danger or sickness, national disaster, and moral degradation was offered by Yahweh to his chosen people of old through his spokesmen, Moses and the prophets. In the Old Testament Yahweh is often hailed by Israel as its "savior" (Is 43:11; 45:15, 21; Hos 13:4; cf. Ps 68:19–20), and he sent to it human agents called "saviors" (Jgs 3:9, 15; 2 Kgs 13:5; Neh 9:27). But Jesus' main teaching was a proclamation of salvation, which prescinded from the election of Israel, which differed at times with some elements of its legal tradition, and which called people to eschatological repentance, in a mode centered in his own person (making acceptance of himself a critical issue in their lives). In him this new and final divine offer of salvation was made to all human beings, to the poor, to the outcasts, to sinners, even to Samaritans and non-Jews who would come to him (depending, indeed, on how one assesses the gospel tradition about Jesus' dealings with non-Jews and Samaritans). (For a more specific form of this salvific teaching, see the answer to question 11.)

b. A second theme of Jesus' preaching was the fundamental validity of what scripture and tradition of old had taught. Jesus repeated the Shema (Deut 6:4, quoted in Mk 12:29) and acknowledged the law in the Old Testament as the source of God's will for human conduct. But he also displayed a new way of allowing it to shape human life and conduct, apart from all casuistry. Not all of Jesus' opposition to the interpretations of the scribes and Pharisees recorded in the canonical gospels can be ascribed to later church-synagogue disputes (see Mk 7:6–7). Related to this fundamental regard for the past is his attitude toward the older forms of piety (prayer, fasting, and almsgiving, Mt 6:1–18) and toward the observance of the sabbath or cultic worship (Mk 2:23–27). But he also insisted on the true and spiritual meaning of such practices and sought to purify them of all too-human attitudes (evasion, hypocrisy, pride) which easily became associated with beliefs and traditions of old.

c. A third theme of Jesus' preaching was a special emphasis on God as Father. His preaching reinforced the traditional Israelite view of God without introducing great novelties into the general picture. Yahweh was still the sole divine being who chose Israel, who gave it the law, and who judged all mankind; his activity was still ruling human existence, guiding all things in its providence. Yahweh was, indeed, the father of Israel (see Deut 32:6; Jer 3:4, 19; 31:9; Is 63:16). But Jesus regarded Yahweh as Father in a special way, calling him "Abba" with an individual, personal nuance (Mk 14:36) and teaching his followers to acknowledge that fatherhood in a new way in prayer (Mt 6:9–13; Lk 11:2–4). This emphasis on God as Father is presented differently in the synoptic and Johannine traditions. In the latter it is a full-blown development. But it is a theme of teaching that in its primitive form is to be traced to Jesus himself.

d. A fourth theme of Jesus' teaching implicitly involved his own person and the role that he was to play in God's new form of salvation. He acted as an agent of Yahweh, as one who could forgive sins and could reinterpret God's word in scripture. Moreover, he coped constantly with the presence of sin in human beings, teaching that God's forgiveness was available for it, precisely through himself. An aspect of his mission can be seen in his willingness to differ with the legal attitudes of old and some widespread beliefs and customs rooted in the Old Testament itself (e.g. his attitude toward adultery [Mt 5:27] and divorce [Mk 10:2–12; Lk 16:18]). Thus, the stance he assumed vis-à-vis Moses, the scriptures, and God revealed much about himself. But it was only an implicit and indirect teaching. Yet the impact that his teaching, his ministry, and his personality made on those who heard him caused many of them to realize that he was presenting himself as someone other than the rest of mankind, and especially other than the rest of contemporary teachers and prophets of old (Mk 1:22).

e. Finally, his teaching included a new emphasis on the role of

Love

love in human life. The Old Testament had insisted on the love of
God and the love of one's neighbor (= one's fellow Jew, Deut 6:4–5;
Lev 19:18). Jesus not only reiterated that insistence (Mk 12:30–31),
but extended it to include even one's enemies (Mt 5:44) and saw in it
the summation of all that was demanded of the pious Israelite (Mt
22:40) and the interiorization of obedience itself. This attitude was
at the root of all other specific demands (about wealth and the poor,
about taxes and Rome, about food or drink and sinners). The Johannine tradition reformulated it in its own way and with its own
emphasis, "In this will all know that you are my disciples, if you
have love for one another" (Jn 13:35).

Some modern interpreters might be inclined to contest one or
other item in the above list, but that merely indicates the difficulty
that faces one in trying to isolate themes of teaching that seem to go
back to the historical Jesus himself. The themes listed above are
formulated in one way or another in the various gospel traditions,
even though not all the possible references for them have been
supplied.

11. What Did Jesus Teach About the Kingdom of God?

The kingship of God is a widely used Old Testament notion,
even though the exact expression, "kingdom of God," which is so
common in one form or another in the New Testament, is rarely
found in the protocanonical writings of the Old Testament. The
closest form is *malkût Yahweh,* "the kingdom of the Lord" (in postexilic 1 Chr 28:5; cf. deuterocanonical Wis 10:10).

a. The kingship of God was a way of expressing Yahweh's sov-
ereignty over humanity, indeed over all of creation. His kingship
denoted a right to be acknowledged as having a dominant influence
in the lives of human creatures (see Pss 22:28; 45:6; 103:19; 145:11,
13; Dan 4:3, 34; 1 Chr 17:14; 29:11). This kingly influence was
understood above all as "salvific" (see §10 above), but it was also

advisory (for he was to be consulted oracularly, in the temple), judicatory (for he was to pass judgment on human and national conduct), and covenantal (for his activity was governed by his sovereign attributes of loving kindness [*ḥesed*], righteousness [*ṣedeq, ṣĕdāqāh*], fidelity [*'ĕmet-*], and mercy [*raḥămîm*]). Especially in the postexilic period Yahweh's kingly activity developed an eschatological aspect, associating it with the "day of the Lord." This development introduced a temporal aspect that promised not only a new intervention of God in human affairs, but also the expectation of a manifestation of his sovereign rule with the establishment of peace, bounty, and harmony for all who would acknowledge his dominion (see Is 2:2–4; 11:6–9; Mic 4:1–4; described with apocalyptic stageprops in Is 24–27; Zech 9–14).

b. The "kingdom of God" (or "of heaven") in Jesus' preaching was a specific way in which he announced the new form of God's salvation. Though there are Qumran expressions that echo the Old Testament's teaching about Yahweh's "kingship" (1QM 12:7; 4QEnGiants[a] 9:6; etc.), the expression "kingdom of God" or of "heaven" (a Jewish periphrasis for "God" in Matthew's gospel) has scarcely been found in these texts. Hence one may ask how frequently it was used in contemporary Palestinian Jewish usage. The emphasis that it receives in Jesus' teaching in the canonical gospels is, therefore, significant. Yet what is striking is that Jesus rarely explained what God's kingdom or kingship meant, more or less taking it for granted that it would be understood. The salvific and temporal (eschatological) aspects of that kingship were stressed, but one notes that in his teaching the kingdom also had a spatial aspect, for one could "enter" it (Mk 9:47; 10:23–25); it could also be "inherited" (Mt 25:34). Apocalyptic stageprops were sometimes used in the preaching of the kingdom so that it could be understood as a sort of visibly manifested irruption of God's rule on a cosmic scale. Such an apocalyptic view of the kingdom helped to prevent a naive understanding of it, as if it were a mere inward reality, an attitude of the human heart. The parables of Jesus, when divested of later eccle-

siastical accretions, often presented the kingdom as a reality of
God's activity among human beings; it was to grow among them,
spread mysteriously, silently, but assuredly, and thus "come" into
its own. The success of the kingdom was assured, even though evil
might appear among its effects (but not as its effect).

c. The major problem in the teaching of Jesus about the kingdom is its eschatology. Are we to understand that Jesus taught that
the "coming" of the kingdom in time was imminent? Here New
Testament interpreters show no agreement; there are almost as
many answers to this question as there are heads that think about it.
The eschatology has been called "realized" (C.H. Dodd), i.e. the
kingdom is already at hand in the person of Jesus. Others view it as
"futurist, but near" (A. Schweitzer, R. Bultmann), i.e. expected as
an imminent inbreaking, and still others as "inaugurated" (J. Jeremias), i.e. in the process of being realized, or both present and future
(W.G. Kümmel). The difficulty here is that the data in the gospel
traditions are such that one cannot fit everything into one simple
classification. Indeed, a writer like Luke has manifestly reformulated some of the sayings because of the delay of the parousia that he
sensed by the time that he wrote. The view of either Kümmel or
Jeremias seems preferable, because the sayings attributed to Jesus
on this point reflect the Old Testament spectrum about the "day of
the Lord" itself. In the long run, one cannot be certain about what
Jesus of Nazareth might have said about the imminence of the
kingdom.

d. In the synoptics Jesus announces a new form of this kingly
activity of God among human beings. In the Lucan gospel he is the
kingdom-preacher par excellence, whereas in the Marcan and
Matthean gospels he is rather presented as the one who establishes
this kingship among human beings both in his word and in his
power. (See Mk 1:14–15; Mt 12:28; note that in the Lucan gospel
John the Baptist is not a kingdom-preacher [compare Mt 3:2; 4:17
with their Lucan counterparts].) The "kingdom" is promised to the
"saints" in Daniel 7:18 (i.e. to corporate Israel); the Matthean Jesus

claims for himself the authority of such a kingdom (Mt 28:18; cf. 16:28), and in the name of all the power that is thus associated with it, he commissions his followers to go forth, make disciples, baptize, and teach in his name (compare the appendix of the Marcan gospel, 16:15). At the end of both the Matthean and the Marcan gospels one sees how Jesus' preaching of the kingdom was given a very specific reformulation in later decades of the early church.

   e. Finally, in some places of the New Testament there is reference to Jesus' own kingdom (e.g. Lk 23:42; Jn 18:36–37; Col 1:13). It is not easy to say to what extent this notion of Jesus' own kingdom is primitive, derived from his teaching; it seems rather to have been born of a more developed christology (cf. 1 Cor 15:24–28) or of a reflection about the relationship of the church (the kingdom of the Son) to the kingdom of God.

12. How Are Jesus' Sayings and Parables To Be Understood, Also His Sermon on the Mount?

   The sayings of Jesus in the synoptic gospels are to be distinguished from those in the Johannine tradition. In the synoptics, the sayings-material is found in general to be of three sorts: isolated sayings, parables, and pronouncements (what R. Bultmann called apophthegms). The last-mentioned are sayings embedded in the narrative tradition of the synoptics, i.e. stories recounted for the sake of the pronouncement or punch-line enshrined in them. An example would be the story about the disciples showing Jesus the Roman denarius with Caesar's likeness on it and Jesus' consequent saying, "Pay to Caesar what is Caesar's and to God what is God's" (Mk 12:17). It is a narrative with dramatic details, which were preserved solely for the sake of the saying. Another example would be the story about the disciples plucking grain in the fields on the sabbath and Jesus' comment to the Pharisees that "the sabbath was made for man, not man for the sabbath" (Mk 2:27).

a. The isolated sayings seem to have floated around early Christian communities; they became detached from their historical contexts and eventually found themselves related to disparate material in different gospels. An example of such sayings would be that about nothing being hidden except to be made manifest, which is derived by Luke (8:17) from the Marcan source (4:22), but which appears again in the Lucan Gospel in another form (12:2), parallel to Matthew 10:26, and hence derived from the "Q" source. As R. Bultmann has pointed out, these isolated sayings can be further subdivided into: (i) wisdom sayings; (ii) prophetic and apocalyptic sayings; (iii) legal sayings and church rules; and (iv) "I" sayings. Some of those in the third category reflect later church problems and have been at least reformulated in terms of these problems, if they do indeed contain some authentic kernel.

b. Highly distinctive of the sayings-material in the synoptic gospels are the parables of Jesus. The Johannine tradition contains no *parabolai,* but on one occasion it passes on a *paroimia,* "a figurative saying" (10:6, used of the preceding saying about the shepherd and the sheepfold [cf. Jn 10:2, 5, 9]). In most cases the synoptic parables are expanded similes in which the story, though fictitious, is true to life (and specifically to life in first century Palestine, with much Semitic coloring). This story teaches a truth (about the kingdom, about God's mercy, about the conduct of disciples) by illustration, but also by introducing a novel or strange twist it teases the hearer to further reflection or consideration. Most parables have only one point of comparison, but a few of them have an allegorizing tendency that identifies various figures or elements in the parable (e.g. the parable of the wicked vineyard-tenants, Mk 12:1–12 and par.). The parables are a didactic device, intended to disclose an obvious aspect of the kingdom, God, or conduct, but they are at times quite subtle. This subtlety often elicited later "interpretations" of the parables, which have even been put on the lips of Jesus himself by the evangelists or by the traditions that they used. Take, for instance, the parable of the sower in Mark 4:3–20. The parable is given in vv. 3–8; v. 9 contains an isolated saying. Verses 10–13 are the early church's explanation about why Jesus used parables, and vv. 14–20 the early church's interpretation of the parable itself. Another example might be the parable of the dishonest manager in Luke 16:1–13. The parable itself is found in vv. 1–8a, but vv. 8b–9, 10–12, 13 supply three allegorical interpretations of the parable, i.e. three different homiletic applications that allegorize details in the story of vv. 1–8a, beyond the real point that the parable was intended to make. See further J. Jeremias, *The Parables of Jesus: Revised Edition* (New York: Scribner, 1963); R.E. Brown, *The Parables of the Gospels* (Glen Rock, N.J.: Paulist, 1963); my *Essays on the Semitic Background of the New Testament,* 161–84.

   c. As interpreters seek to understand the sayings, parables, and pronouncements of the synoptic tradition, they are not interested solely in stripping off the editorial accretions in order to recover the original logia or sayings and parables of Jesus. They also seek to understand the gospel context in which the sayings are now enshrined as well as what these might mean to a modern reader. Often enough the redactional work of the evangelist has a theological thrust or an interpretive nuance that may be as important for Christians of our generation as the original sayings of Jesus themselves. Take, for example, the Lucan addition of "the Holy Spirit" to Jesus' saying about prayer being answered: "If you then who are evil know how to give good gifts to your own children, how much more will the Father from heaven give the Holy Spirit to those who ask him" (Lk 11:13). Contrast the more original "Q" form of the saying in Matthew 7:11 ("If you then who are evil know how to give good gifts to your children, how much more will your Father . . . give good things to those who ask him"). Recall too the Lucan emphasis on the role of the Spirit in Christian life. Some readers may be reluctant to admit this sort of "tampering" with the words of Jesus, even by an evangelist under inspiration. They might prefer to think that perhaps Jesus uttered the saying in a variant way on a different occasion. That solution is, of course, always theoretically possible, but given the complexity and frequency of the phenomenon, that solution is simply unconvincing and scarcely applicable to the problem.

d. In turning to the Johannine sayings, one encounters sayings that are independent of the synoptics and derived from a tradition that makes Jesus speak quite differently. Bultmann once distinguished three sources of the Johannine gospel: (1) a signs-source (the narratives of Jesus' miracles); (2) the revelatory-discourse source; and (3) the passion and resurrection stories. The Johannine sayings of Jesus would have been derived from the revelatory-discourse source. Though there are many difficulties with that analysis, and Bultmann's source-theory of the Johannine gospel is widely questioned today, the distinction that he made at least alerts the reader to the variety of material that is found in the fourth gospel. Rather than being derived from an earlier written source, the speeches are the composition of an author (and an editor [at least one]) who has structured the dialogues and narratives to his own purpose(s). The speeches are often repetitious and probably reflect different forms of the same discourse, which have been incorporated into the gospel. They are not, however, fabrications out of whole cloth. What may be historical in them has been overlaid with much else (especially with interpretive meditation and speculative hindsight).

The diversity of the Johannine speeches from the sayings-material in the synoptics is not merely a matter of language in the sense of style or grammar, but rather in the realm of concepts and images. The Johannine speeches are characterized by a dualism of light and darkness, truth and falsehood, above and below; by a contrast of father and son; by numerous "I am" sayings, which differ from the "I" sayings of the synoptics (by the absolute use of "I am" or the use of it with symbolic predicates); and by highly distinctive images for salvation (water of life, bread of life, light of the world, gate of the sheepfold, etc.). What the Johannine speeches manifest in the long run is an understanding of Jesus, with a "high" christology, for which the synoptics showed little interest. Though "the discourses consist of traditional sayings and explanatory developments" (R.E. Brown), there is certainly more of the latter than of the former. For an interpretation of the early church context in which the Johannine gospel came into being, see R.E. Brown, *The Community of the Beloved Disciple* (New York: Paulist, 1979).

e. As for the sermon on the mount (Mt 5:1–7:27), we recognize today that Matthew has here preserved for us a significant body of Jesus' sayings. Its ninety-nine verses stand in contrast, however, to the thirty verses of its Lucan parallel, the sermon on the plain (6:20–49). Both preserve the recollection of a significant, prolonged discourse that Jesus delivered toward the beginning of his Galilean ministry. (The Marcan sermon in parables, 4:1–33, may reflect the same recollection.) The Lucan and Matthean sermons are related: they have the same basic theme (the uprightness demanded of disciples by the kingship of God), the same exordium (beatitudes, though differing in number), the same conclusion (the parable of the two houses), and the same generic setting (reference to a mountain [Mt 5:1; Lk 6:12, 17], and to the beginning of the ministry). They are both followed by the cure of a centurion's servant (Mt 8:5–13; Lk 7:1–10). The longer Matthean form of the sermon is explained in two ways: (1) Luke, writing for a predominantly Gentile Christian community, has omitted much material that would have had meaning only in a specifically Jewish-Christian setting (e.g. what corresponds to Mt 5:17, 19–20, 21–24, 27–28, 33–39a,43; 6:1–8, 16–18; 7:6, 15); and (2) Matthew has introduced many sayings which Luke uses elsewhere, e.g. to expand his travel account (Lk 9:51–18:14). This difference of treatment illustrates how these two evangelists have made use of the "Q" material, by inserting isolated sayings and parables into parts of their gospels that they deemed important.

The structure of the Matthean sermon on the mount is carefully worked out: (i) exordium (5:3–16, beatitudes, etc.); (ii) thesis (5:17–20, esp. v. 20, which gives structure to the rest of the sermon); (iii) the uprightness of the scribes (5:21–48, six legal antitheses); (iv) the uprightness of the Pharisees (6:1–18, sayings about three prac-

tices of Pharisaic piety: almsgiving, prayer, fasting); and (v) the
uprightness of Jesus' disciples (6:19–7:27, a series of isolated sayings
strung together, describing the transformation of human life demanded by God's new form of kingship). Many of the sayings in the
sermon on the mount are to be traced back to Jesus himself, but
some have clear Matthean formulation, e.g. the exceptive phrase in
the prohibition of divorce (5:32; cf. 19:9), which is found only in
Matthew. (One may contrast the earliest form of the prohibition in 1
Corinthians 7:10–11; the most primitive form in Luke 16:18; and
the adapted form in Mark 10:11–12, all of them, however, absolute
in their formulation of the prohibition, i.e. without an exception.—
See further my article, "The Matthean Divorce Texts and Some
New Palestinian Evidence," TS *37* [1976] 197–226; reprinted in *To
Advance the Gospel: New Testament Studies* [New York: Crossroad,
1981] 79–111.) Similarly Matthean is the formulation "Our Father
in heaven" in 6:9 (compare 5:16, 45, 48; 6:1, 14; but also contrast Lk
11:2, "Father!").

In all, the sermon is neither a perfectionist's code, nor an in-
terim ethic, nor an exposé of the impossible ideal, nor a utopian
dream, nor a new torah. It represents rather the Matthean Jesus'
radical demands for the transformation of human life in God's
kingdom.

13. How Are the Gospel Accounts of Jesus' Miracles To Be Understood?

Once again, we must distinguish the synoptic and Johannine
traditions about Jesus' miracles. In the synoptic tradition four different types of miracle stories are recorded: (1) healings (possibly
fifteen of them); (2) exorcisms (five); (3) resuscitations (two); and (4)
nature miracles (six, with one of them a "would be" [Matt 17:24–27,
the story about the coin in the fish's mouth, the outcome of which
we never learn]). In the Johannine tradition, seven miracles are re-

counted in the so-called Book of Signs (chapters 1–12), and another in the appendix (chapter 21). Of these, three are healings, one is a resuscitation, and four are nature miracles. Among the latter, two have parallels in the synoptics: the feeding of five thousand (6:1–13; cf. Mk 6:30–44) and Jesus' walking on the water (6:16–21; cf. Mk 6:45–52). In John's gospel there is no account of an exorcism. Does this represent an advanced understanding of exorcisms? See John 10:21 for a query about a demon; but otherwise there is *not once a* mention in the fourth gospel of a dumb or unclean spirit.

a. What is significant here is the independent, multiple attestation of a tradition about Jesus' performance of miraculous deeds. Both the synoptics and John independently testify about Jesus' miracles. Thus the miracles of Jesus form part of traditions that considered them no less important than the words of Jesus. Indeed, miracles are part of the earlier (pre-Stage III) tradition, and one finds the evidence for Jesus as a miracle-worker to be as old as that for him as one who uttered significant sayings and parables. In this regard, it might be well to recall the extrabiblical testimony of Josephus about Jesus as a *paradoxōn ergōn poiētēs,* "a worker of wondrous deeds" (*Ant.* 18.3,3 §63).

b. Further significance is seen in the terms used for these actions, since they are never called "miracles" (a word derived from a later Latin theological tradition, *miraculum,* and predicated of them, often with anachronistic nuances). In the synoptics they are usually called *dynameis,* "deeds of might" (or of "power") (Mk 6:2, 5; Lk 10:13; 19:37; Mt 13:54). In John they are rather referred to as *erga,* "works, deeds" (e.g. 5:36; 10:25, 32) or even *sēmeia,* "signs" (e.g. 2:11; 4:54; 9:16). The latter term immediately shifts our attention from them as deeds that might transcend what has been called the laws of nature to their religious value and significance, which is invariably found in the gospel stories that recount them. The former term, *dynameis,* suggests rather something about the person of Jesus and the kingdom that he announces. There is thus a christological aspect to them.

Luke, however, has added an apologetic nuance to them, when he writes in Acts 2:22 about Jesus of Nazareth as "a man (*andra*) attested to you by God with mighty works, wonders, and signs." Yet not even Luke presses on to the conclusion that is so often drawn from this way of considering them, viz. to the divinity of Jesus, as did Melito of Sardis (*Frg.* 7; PG 5. 1221; he died ca. A.D. 190), or at least to the plausibility of believing in it, as in traditional apologetics. For Luke, Jesus is rather God's attested agent, later described in the same speech of Peter as "Lord and Christ" (2:36). In the other synoptics, however, the miracles of Jesus serve much more to announce that the kingship of God is now breaking anew into human history and into that of Palestinian Judaism in particular. They are the concrete evidence that a new understanding of God's kingship is authentic.

c. For modern readers the miracle stories of the gospels raise the problem of credibility. Though the tradition about Jesus' miracles is authentic, that does not mean that the historicity of every detail of a gospel miracle is guaranteed. In this connection we should recall the following. (1) Some of the stories have acquired folkloric accretions. An indication of this is given in the most fantastic of the miracle stories, that of the Gerasene demoniac and the swine (Mk 5:1–20). The trace of such accretion is present in the ending, "And he went away and began to tell in all the Decapolis how much Jesus had done for him. . . ." Moreover, the accounts of this miracle defy all attempts to locate the scene near a sea (Mk 5:13, which Luke corrects to "the lake" [8:33]). The manuscript tradition gives three sites for it, two of which are far from Lake Tiberias: *Gerasa* (= modern Jerash, about thirty miles to the southeast of the lake) and *Gadara* (about six miles to the southeast). A third site, *Gergesa,* supposedly on the eastern edge of the lake, is poorly attested in the manuscript tradition and otherwise historically unknown. This name is often traced to Origen, but probably comes from an earlier tradition, which may have been invented precisely to solve the problem of location. Even if one were to admit with Johannes Weiss that the paroxysm accompanying the exorcism set the herd of swine in motion, they would have become the most energetic hogs in history to reach such a cliff. The story is of the sort that one finds in the apocryphal gospel tradition of the infancy of Jesus; it represents a certain climax of the miraculous tradition, which has invaded even the canonical gospels themselves. By contrast, most of the other accounts of Jesus' miracles are told with a sobriety that has often been called striking.

(2) In several accounts of healings or exorcisms one finds clear instances of protological thinking. (Thinking is said to be "proto-logical" when it seeks to give an explanation of something in a primitive, imprecise form.) Persons afflicted with what we would call today mental disturbances were regarded as possessed, because observers were unable to analyze or diagnose properly the causes of the maladies in question. Consequently, they ascribed the afflictions to demons. Mark 9:14–29 tells of the exorcism of a boy whose father said that he has a "dumb spirit"; in the Matthean parallel (17:15) he is described as "moonstruck" (*selēniazetai* [a verb cognate to the noun *selēnē,* "moon"]). Anyone reading that story today recognizes the boy to have been epileptic. Here we are dealing with what has been called "demon-sickness" (or "demon-disasters"). A demon is invoked to explain the cause of the sickness or disaster that people of that time could not otherwise explain or diagnose properly. Their knowledge of the causes of illness was not that of modern medicine. Recall, too, how Jesus is said to "rebuke" the fever of Simon's mother-in-law (Lk 4:39; but cf. Mk 1:31; Mt 8:15), i.e. he is regarded as having rebuked the spirit protologically considered to be causing the high fever. Similarly, he "rebukes" the winds and the waves (Mk 4:39 and par.), i.e. he is regarded as having rebuked the demon or spirit causing the squall. Undoubtedly Jesus shared some of the protological thinking himself, being a child of his time.

(3) Having thus demythologized some of the fantasy and the protological thinking found in some of the miracle stories, we are left with a still more basic problem. For if, in reality, Jesus did not

exorcise a demon, but cured a mentally-ill person, was it less of a miracle? Some New Testament interpreters (such as R. Bultmann and certain of his followers) have sought to write off the entire tradition of Jesus' miracles in the New Testament by ascribing them to the Hellenistic background of the gospels and to the concern of early Christians to depict Jesus as another *theios anēr,* "divine man," or thaumaturge of the Greco-Roman world. True, one can find at times parallels in contemporary literature to some of the miracle stories in the gospels (even with a close resemblance in form). But the extent to which the miracle stories, as we have them, are to be wholly attributed to Hellenistic Christianity is precisely the difficulty. The *Genesis Apocryphon* of Qumran Cave 1 knows of a tradition about Abram's curing the pharaoh Zoan of an affliction caused by an evil spirit sent because the pharaoh had carried off Sarai, Abram's wife; this he did by laying on his hands and praying for the pharaoh (20:29; cf. Lk 4:40–41). This example reveals that miraculous cures were as much at home in Palestinian Jewish literature as in the larger Greco-Roman world. And the historian Josephus, a Palestinian Jew, had no difficulty in accepting the miraculous in Old Testament accounts because they were for him manifestations of God's "providence" (*pronoia*) and "power" (*dynamis*); see *Ant.* 2.16,1 §336.

Paul's letters, however, show no interest in the miraculous activity of Jesus, even though he did not fail to speak of such acts in his own experience and life (see 2 Cor 12:12; cf. 1 Cor 12:10, 28, 29; Gal 3:5). But then, how little interest does Paul show in anything in the earthly career of Jesus prior to the last supper! Luke's references to Jesus' miracles in Acts (2:22; 10:38) do not represent an independent testimony about them; they are clearly dependent on his own gospel.

(4) Several other aspects of the miracle stories of the gospels have to be considered. (i) Whether the devil, the Pharisees, Herod, or just ordinary people sought signs or miracles from Jesus as evidence that he was sent by God, the New Testament writers attest

that he refused to perform them either in his own interest or to satisfy the curiosity of his contemporaries (see Mk 6:5a; 8:11–13; 15:31–32; Mt 4:5–7; Lk 4:9–12; 23:8–9). (ii) The gospels never depict Jesus miraculously punishing human beings, as Peter does to Ananias and Sapphira (Acts 5:1–11), or Paul to Elymas the magician (Acts 13:10–11), or the angel to Zechariah (Lk 1:20), all, significantly enough, in Luke-Acts. In cursing the barren fig tree, Jesus is portrayed using his power on a non-human creature, in an act symbolic of the fate of Jerusalem's house of prayer (see Mk 11:12–25; cf. Mt 21:18–22, significantly omitted by Luke). (iii) One has to recognize the symbolic value and meaning of the miracles of Jesus which are recounted. I do not refer to the specific symbolism associated with one or other miracle (e.g. the way that the evangelists have, with hindsight, made the accounts of the multiplication of the loaves foreshadow the eucharist). I mean rather the symbolism of the conquest of evil; the miracles thus announce a new form of God's regal activity in the conquest of evil afflicting his people. Sin, physical or mental illness, disasters in nature, even death itself, are forms of the power of evil in human life. Jesus is depicted possessing the power of the kingdom, which clearly makes known that a counterforce is present among human beings to cope with such evil. (iv) An element that is so frequently associated with the miracles of Jesus in both the synoptics and John is faith, not a belief in demons, but rather faith in the salvific power that is now manifest in Jesus, the agent of Yahweh. In such gospel stories it is not yet (in Stage I) full Christian faith. Such faith would presuppose the resurrection of Jesus: faith in the risen Christ. It is rather an awareness of and trust in God's providence manifest in Jesus.

d. In the long run, the greatest difficulty sensed today with the gospel miracles is a philosophic one: Can God or does God intervene in human history by such extraordinary means? This is a philosophic problem born of an outlook which stems from the *Aufklärung* or enlightenment. To try to solve that problem, using examples drawn from ancient texts or the early Christian heritage, is misguided. The gospel accounts, of which the miracle stories form part of the warp and woof, were not composed to answer such a problem. Moreover, a modern philosophical interpretation of the world in which we live cannot be the answer to an historical question. After all, some modern people do believe in God's miraculous intervention in human history.

14. How Are Jesus' Words to Simon Peter at Caesarea Philippi To Be Understood?

The question is concerned with the scene of Peter acknowledging Jesus' messiahship in the synoptic tradition (Mk 8:27–33; Mt 16:13–23; Lk 9:18–22). Only Mark and Matthew mention the locale of the episode: Caesarea Philippi. Luke omits all reference to locale, only placing the episode toward the end of Jesus' Galilean ministry (9:18–20), shortly before he begins his journey from Galilee to Jerusalem (9:51). It is, in fact, the first episode with which Luke resumes his use of Marcan material after the so-called "big omission" of this material in his gospel (= Mark 6:45–8:26). Since Caesarea Philippi was outside of Galilee, Luke would not want to admit that Jesus was there. Given the literary build-up of his gospel and its geographical perspective, in which Jesus moves resolutely from his Galilean ministry to Jerusalem, the city of destiny, an episode situated at Caesarea Philippi would be an added distraction.

a. Many commentators regard John 6:67–71 as a related form of the same tradition. The episode there is located in the synagogue of Capernaum, again in Galilee (6:59), and Peter acknowledges Jesus to be, not the messiah, but "Lord" and the "Holy One of God." Given its general relation to the Galilean ministry, there may be some connection between this Johannine confession of Peter and the synoptic form as found in Mark.

b. In the synoptic form Jesus asks his disciples, "Who do people say I am?" Having received various answers (John the Baptist,

Elijah, one of the prophets [Matthew adds, "Jeremiah"]), Jesus then asks the disciples, "Who do you say I am?" Peter speaks up. In Mark 8:29 he acknowledges Jesus to be "the messiah" (or "Christ," *ho christos*); in Luke 9:20, "God's messiah" (or "the Christ of God"); in Matthew 16:16, "the messiah (or Christ), the Son of the living God." The tradition about Peter's confession has obviously grown.

c. In Mark (8:30) and Luke (9:21) Jesus immediately charges the disciples to tell this to no one and proceeds to make the first announcement of his passion, death, and resurrection (as the Son of Man). Though Luke omits it, Mark adds Peter's uncomprehending protest, to which Jesus replies with an epithet for Peter and a rebuke: Peter is identified as Satan and "not on the side of God but of human beings."

d. In the oldest form of the tradition about Peter's confession (Mk 8:27–33), there is thus an acknowledgement by Peter, the spokesman for the disciples, that Jesus is the messiah. The fact that Jesus forbids his disciples to repeat that acknowledgement and that he counters it with a corrective saying about his own fate reveals that he did not accept the implications of the title as used by Peter. The extent to which Peter (and other disciples) would have considered Jesus to be a messiah in a political sense is difficult for us to ascertain today. Certainly Peter's acknowledgement of Jesus as messiah cannot be understood in Stage I of the gospel tradition with all the connotations of the title in Stages II or III (see §4h above). Peter's confession would have to be taken as an indication of a breakthrough of some sort in the disciples' awareness about who Jesus was, though only in an inceptive way. Yet that title in no way implies an allegiance to Jesus that would keep Peter from eventually denying him (14:66–72) or the disciples from deserting him (14:50–52). For the connotation, see further §22a below.

e. As used in the Marcan gospel, Peter's confession and Jesus' subsequent sayings form a turning point in the literary structure of that writing. Up to this point (inclusive) Jesus imposes silence on those who would use titles of him; after that point the use of titles changes, and the climax of the revelation about him in the Marcan gospel is reached when a pagan Roman centurion declares about the crucified Jesus, "Surely, this man was the Son of God!" (15:39).

f. The Lucan use of Marcan material is significant for three things: (1) The title is slightly expanded: Jesus is "God's messiah" (9:20). However, this is not radically different from the Marcan confession. (2) Luke omits all reference to Peter's protest and Jesus' rebuke. This fits in with the general tendency in the Lucan gospel, in which the disciples are not portrayed as deserting Jesus. (In fact, even at the crucifixion among those standing not far off from Jesus are not only the women who had followed him from Galilee, but "all his acquaintances" [*hoi gnōstoi,* masculine! (23:49)], so that his disciples have not deserted him.) Peter will, indeed, deny Jesus in the Lucan gospel, but Jesus will pray for him (22:32), and he will be converted. (3) The confession of Peter plays a different role in the Lucan gospel, not enhancing Peter so much, as it does in Matthew, but supplying an important christological assertion. Because of the "big omission" (see above), Peter's confession comes in Luke's sequence on the heels of Herod's crucial question, "Who is this about whom I hear such talk?" (9:9). It thus proves to be one of several christological answers given to that question in chapter 9, which is a peculiarly Lucan refashioning of the synoptic tradition. (See further my commentary, *The Gospel according to Luke* [AB 28-28A; Garden City, NY: Doubleday, 1981, 1985] 756–58.)

g. Matthew too has made use of the Marcan story; its parallel is found in 16:13–16a, 20–23 (with Peter's protest and Jesus' rebuke retained). But the Matthean gospel has in this instance some additional material (vv. 16b–19), which further expands (significantly) Peter's confession: Jesus is not only "the messiah," but "the Son of the living God." To this acknowledgement Jesus now replies with an admission that Peter's insight has been granted by God ("Flesh and blood have not revealed this to you, but my Father who is in heaven"). Jesus then bestows on Simon a title, *Petros* (masculine), "Rock," and promises to build his church unshakably on "this

rock" (*petra,* feminine) and give him authority in it. Having pronounced a beatitude over Simon Peter and promised him a significant role or function, Jesus charges his disciples to tell no one that he
is the messiah (16:20), thus resuming the Marcan form of the story
with Peter's protest and Jesus' rebuke. In the present Matthean context the retention of this material clashes with the beatitude and the
promises.

Verses 16b–19 are an addition to the story inherited from
Mark, added by the evangelist who is using material from another
part of the gospel tradition. In John 21:15–17 the risen Christ, having appeared to seven disciples in Galilee at Lake Tiberias, confers
authority on Simon Peter as he commissions him (three times over)
to feed his sheep. Whereas former generations of interpreters often
distinguished the *promise* of a Petrine function to Simon (in
Matthew 16) and the *conferral* of it (in John 21), modern interpreters regard the additional material in Matthew 16:16b–19 as a
variant in the synoptic gospel tradition of that in the Johannine
scene. Matthew would then have retrojected an episode from the
tradition about appearances of the risen Christ into the public ministry itself. The acknowledgement of Jesus as "the Son of the living
God" is certainly more plausible on the lips of Peter after his denial
and the experience of the resurrection than it is at Caesarea Philippi.
Such a christological title as "Son of the living God" could readily
have been joined to the other one, "the messiah," which was more
suited to the ministry itself, thus producing in Matthew 16:16 a
double confession on the lips of Peter. This post-resurrection matrix
for the material in vv. 16b–19 also provides a plausible setting for
the beatitude pronounced over Peter by Jesus and for the church-
founding promises made to him, a setting far more plausible than in
the ministry itself.

h. This theory would also provide a plausible explanation for
what has always been a major problem in the episode of Peter's
confession: If Jesus had said all this (Mt 16:16–19) to Simon at
Caesarea Philippi, how could Mark (and Luke) have failed to find

any trace of these words in the tradition about the Galilean ministry? If Matthew 16:13–19 were the more correct record of what
had happened at Caesarea Philippi, how could the tradition have
arisen in such a truncated form as that now found in Mark 8 and
Luke 9? Rather, it seems likely that Matthew has followed his custom of adding things, in this case, to the sayings of both Simon Peter
and Jesus.

i. Lastly, this theory also explains why the word "church" (*ekklēsia*) appears only in the Matthean form of the episode, and nowhere else in the gospel tradition (save, again, in a Matthean passage, 18:17). Neither Mark, nor Luke (in his gospel), nor John ever
portrays Jesus speaking of his community of followers as "the
church." See further §25 below.

j. In the Matthean gospel the expanded episode (16:13–23)
joins two others in which material has been added by the evangelist
and all of which enhance the Petrine role: Matthew 14:22–33
(Peter's walking on the waters, to be compared with Mark 6:45–52
[omitted by Luke]) and Matthew 17:24–27 (the finding of a coin in
the fish's mouth, an episode exclusive to Matthew). All three episodes relate Peter closely to Jesus. They describe the Petrine function in a manner that is unique to this gospel. It has, in turn, had a
marked emphasis on the developing ecclesiology of the early church
beyond that of any other gospel. See further R.E. Brown et al. (eds.),
Peter in the New Testament (New York: Paulist; Minneapolis: Augsburg, 1973) 75–107.

15. How Are Jesus' Words and Actions at the Last Supper To Be Understood?

The question refers to the passages in 1 Corinthians 11:23–25;
Mark 14:17–25; Matthew 26:20–29; Luke 22:14–38; John 13:1–
17:26, even though the name "last supper" is never found in any of
them. That is a development out of the reference to Jesus' "dining"

(1 Cor 11:25), which two verses earlier is dated to "the night on which he was betrayed." Cf. John 13:1–2 for another way of phrasing it. The nature of that meal that Jesus took with his apostles shortly before his arrest, trial, and death is, however, variously described in the New Testament.

a. The Johannine gospel restricts Jesus' actions at that meal to the washing of the feet of the disciples (apart from his giving a dipped morsel of food to Judas, 13:26). The washing of the feet was a symbolic act not understood at the time by those present, but intended by the evangelist as an "example" to portray Jesus' fundamental attitude of lowly service to those whom the Father had given him (his chosen followers): "that you too should do as I have done to you" (13:15). This act, unrecorded in the earlier tradition about the supper, either Pauline or synoptic, is evidently intended to give a symbolic summation of the whole life of Jesus.

The Johannine account likewise depicts Jesus uttering several lengthy discourses (14:1–16:33 [composite]; 17:1–26). These are again unknown to Paul and the synoptics (Lk 22:21–38 includes four sayings of Jesus in his account, quite different in content, however, from the lengthy discourses of the Johannine Jesus). This Johannine tradition about Jesus' words at the "last supper" (interpreting his mission, his relation to the Father, the coming of the Spirit-Paraclete, and the mission of the apostles) obviously developed independently of the other early traditions about that meal.

b. The earliest reference in the New Testament to the "last supper" (and what soon grew out of it) is found in 1 Corinthians (written about A.D. 56), where Paul, even before he recounts what Jesus did and said at it, speaks of a participation of Christians in "the table of the Lord" (10:21). He thus refers to what was already a well-established ritual custom among Corinthian Christians. At it they shared in a "cup of blessing" (10:16a), which Paul now interprets as "a participation in the blood of Christ" (v. 16b) and in a "breaking of bread" (v. 16c), which is "a participation in the body of Christ" (v. 16d): "All partake of the one bread" (10:17). Thus Paul alludes to a Christian rite, which he even compares with "sacrifices" of "the people of Israel" (10:18) and other sacrifices of "pagans" (10:20), as he emphasizes the idea of partnership or participation of those involved in it.

To what rite Paul alludes becomes clear when he refers to it as "the Lord's supper" (11:20) and shortly thereafter recounts its origin in actions and words of Jesus at a supper taken before his arrest. In 11:23–25 he thus records the earliest account of the institution of that rite: how on the night of his betrayal, Jesus took bread, gave thanks (to God), broke it, and said, "This is my body, which is for you," adding the directive to reenact this action in memory of him. Similarly, "after supper" he took a cup of wine and said of it, "This cup is the new covenant in my blood," repeating the directive. This tradition Paul inherited and passed on (1 Cor 11:23a).

c. Independently, the synoptic evangelists were heirs to a similar "last supper" tradition (Mk 14:22–25; Mt 26:26–29; Lk 22:17–20). These passages belong to a larger context in which disciples are sent by Jesus to make preparations for the celebration of the Passover at the beginning of the "first day of Unleavened Bread" (Mk 14:12; Mt 26:17; Lk 22:7). In these accounts the Matthean closely follows the Marcan, whereas the Lucan is tributary to a separate tradition, which is in some respects similar to the Pauline (e.g. the reference to the cup "after supper" [22:20] and the inclusion of the memento-directive [22:19c]). But in other respects the Lucan account is quite independent too of the Pauline (e.g. the mention of two cups [22:17, 20]; the relation of the eating of the Passover [-lamb] to Jesus' own suffering [22:15]). (N.B. Recent Greek manuscript-discoveries make it clear that vv. 19bc–20 were part of the genuine Lucan text; so they are to be retained in translations and not relegated to footnotes, as has been done at times in this century by those translators who have followed a fad once started by Westcott and Hort in 1881 [see Nestle-Aland[26]].)

d. A classic problem must now be mentioned. In the Johan-

Jo. - eve of Passover
Syn - Passover itself

nine gospel Jesus eats the "last supper" with his disciples at sundown at the beginning of the Parasceve (the preparation day before the Passover itself, 18:28b). But in the synoptics it is eaten at sundown as the Passover begins (Mk 14:16c; Mt 26:19b; Lk 22:13c) or at the beginning of the "(first) day of Unleavened Bread." This difference of dating raises the question, "Was the 'last supper' a Passover meal or not?" According to all four evangelists the meal would have taken place on what we call Thursday evening. But was the Thursday night/Friday a Passover (as the synoptics suggest) or a Parasceve (as the Johannine tradition suggests)? Which tradition, then, is correct, the synoptic or the Johannine? It is difficult to say. Attempts to explain the difference of the day in the two traditions by appealing to the use of different calendars, Essene and Pharisaic (or temple), only raise more problems than they solve. It might be worth recalling that the baraita of the Babylonian Talmud (*Sanhedrin* 43a [referred to in §2a above]) mentions that Yeshu was "hanged on the eve of Passover."

Early Christian theology may have dictated the preferences of those who fashioned the differing pre-gospel traditions that were used by the evangelists. We can only speculate about such preferences. On the one hand, the synoptic tradition may have preferred to portray Jesus eating the "last supper" with his disciples as an interpretive replacement of the Passover meal of old (this preference emerges most clearly in Luke 22:15–16). On the other hand, the motif of Jesus as "the lamb of God" (Jn 1:36) may have contributed to the preference to depict his dying on the cross about the time on the Parasceve when the lambs were being slaughtered for the coming sundown meal at the beginning of Passover. Hence even though the "last supper" would not have been eaten at the beginning of Passover in the Johannine tradition, an association of Jesus' death with the Passover lamb may be suggested. Recall further the typical sense given to Numbers 9:12 (the prohibition to break a bone of the Passover lamb) when it is used to explain why Jesus' legs were not broken, but his side pierced instead in John 19:33–36. Recall too the Pauline allusion to an ancient tradition that already regarded Christ as "our Passover (*or* Passover lamb)" in 1 Corinthians 5:7.

In either case a strong early Christian tradition, reflected in the Pauline and synoptic accounts, traced the celebration of the eucharistic liturgy to the words and actions of Jesus at the "last supper." Even the venerable name "eucharist" for that liturgy is derived from a participle used in the Pauline and synoptic accounts to describe one of Jesus' actions, *eucharistēsas,* "having given thanks" (1 Cor 11:24; Mk 14:23; Mt 26:27; Lk 22:17, 19).

e. However, what has been retained about Jesus' words and actions at the "last supper" in these varied traditions has been preserved with nuances, and with neither unanimity nor word-for-word exactitude. Whereas the Pauline and the synoptic tradition clearly relates the eucharist to that meal, the Johannine does not; and the traditions differ as to whether it was a Passover meal or not. Moreover, the words of institution recorded in the Pauline and synoptic accounts are not uniformly transmitted (see below). It is generally thought that the divergences reflect formulas already in use in different early liturgical settings, which were no longer primarily concerned with the *ipsissima verba Iesu,* but with the significance of Jesus' words and actions at the "last supper" for his followers and all subsequent generations. The Marcan-Matthean formula possibly reflects a Jerusalemite usage, the Pauline-Lucan possibly an Antiochene. In any case, it is puzzling why more fidelity to the wording or unanimity would not have been displayed. One might have thought that the early Christians would have retained exactly at least this part of the gospel tradition. Yet the situation itself offers a salutary corrective to our modern, twentieth century preoccupations about just what did happen.

f. When we consider the words uttered by Jesus at the "last supper" over the bread and the cup of wine, we must note, *first of all,* the diversity of the tradition. Here are the various reports of Jesus' words over the bread (*arton*):

1 Corinthians 11:24
"This is my body which is for you" (*RSV*).
Touto mou estin to sōma to hyper hymōn
[Note the order of the Greek words!]

Mark 14:22
"Take; this is my body" (*RSV*).
Labete, touto estin to sōma mou

Matthew 26:26
"Take, eat; this is my body" (*RSV*).
Labete, phagete touto estin to sōma mou

Luke 22:19
"This is my body, which is given for you" (*RSV*).
Touto estin to sōma mou to hyper hymōn didomenon

These words of Jesus over the bread may be reflected in the Johannine tradition about the bread of life:

John 6:51
"I am the living bread which came down from heaven; if any one eats of this bread, he will live forever; and the bread which I shall give for the life of the world is my flesh" (*RSV*).
Egō eimi ho artos ho zōn ho ek tou ouranou katabas. ean tis phagē ek toutou tou artou, zēsei eis ton aiōna. kai ho artos de hon egō dōsō hē sarx mou estin hyper tēs tou kosmou zōēs.

Here are the various reports of Jesus' words over the cup of wine:

1 Corinthians 11:25
"This cup is the new covenant in my blood" (*RSV*).

Touto to potērion hē kainē diathēkē estin en tō emō haimati

Mark 14:24
"This is my blood of the covenant, which is poured out for many" (*RSV*).
Touto estin to haima mou tēs diathēkēs to ekchynnomenon hyper pollōn

Matthew 26:27–28
"Drink of it, all of you; for this is my blood of the covenant, which is poured out for many for the forgiveness of sins" (*RSV*).
Piete ex autou pantes, touto gar estin to haima mou tēs diathēkēs to peri pollōn ekchynnomenon eis aphesin hamartiōn

Luke 22:20
"This cup which is poured out for you is the new covenant in my blood" (*RSV*). [Words over the second cup; cf. 22:17b]
Touto to potērion hē kainē diathēkē estin en tō haimati mou to hyper hymōn ekchynnomenon

Confronted with such diversity, one may ask, "Well, just what formula did Jesus use on that historic occasion?" Who can say? And the problem is compounded when one recalls that what we have is almost certainly varying forms of a Greek translation of what he probably uttered in Aramaic.

Second, in these formulas there is an element that identifies Jesus' body and blood with the bread and wine and also an interpretive element. One should learn to distinguish the two.

f. The words uttered by Jesus over the bread and the cup of wine in the Pauline and synoptic accounts of the supper may be an

imitation of those uttered by the head of the Jewish family that ate
together the Passover meal: "This is the bread of affliction which our
fathers had to eat as they came out of Egypt" (see J. Jeremias, *Eucharistic Words of Jesus* [Philadelphia: Fortress, 1977] 54–57; cf. G.
Dalman, *Jesus-Jeshua: Studies in the Gospels* [New York: Ktav,
1971] 139). Such an interpretive formula as the background for
"This is my body" or even "This is my blood of the covenant"
would supply a Passover nuance to the words of institution. An
objection, however, has often been raised: The synoptic (and Pauline) accounts fail to mention the essentials of the Passover meal
(the lamb, the haroseth-sauce, etc.). This objection has its own problems, in that we are not sure how *to pascha* in the New Testament is
to be translated. Should it be merely "the Passover" or, "the Passover lamb" (Mk 14:12, 14, 16; Mt 26:17, 19; Lk 22:7, 11, 13, 15)?
Cf. Mt 26:23. Such elements would support the Passover connotation of the instituted eucharist.

g. The eucharistic words of Jesus have an element of ambiguity. Does the Greek verb *estin* in these formulas mean "is really" (as
the verb "to be" denotes in Matthew 3:17; 10:2; 13:55; 14:2) or "is
symbolically/spiritually" (as in John 10:7, 11; 11:25, etc.)? On the
purely philological level, it could mean either. Relying on such Pauline interpretive passages as 1 Corinthians 11:26–29, early Christian
tradition interpreted the verb in the former, realistic sense. It was
only in the middle ages that this realistic sense began to be questioned. However, that realistic sense, which is a distinct philological
possibility, means that Jesus would have identified the bread and the
wine with his own body and blood.

h. In some of the accounts Jesus' words include an interpretive
element, which adds a soteriological dimension to the eucharist.
Whereas the Marcan and Matthean formulas simply identify the
bread with Jesus' body, 1 Corinthians 11:24 adds, ". . . my body,
which is for you" (a later [harmonizing?] correction is found in some
Pauline manuscripts: "which is *broken* for you"); and Luke 22:19b
has ". . . my body, which is *given for you.*" Similarly, in the case of

the cup of wine, the Pauline formula is the simplest (including a reference to the covenant in the identifying words). But the synoptic formulas all agree at least in adding the interpretive words about the blood being "poured out for" (you/many). In both instances (of the words over the bread and over the cup of wine) one would be inclined to regard the leaner (Pauline) form as the more primitive (and possibly original), whereas the expanded forms would find a plausible matrix in the early church's reflection on the significance of the eucharistic elements as related to the death of Jesus (i.e. added by hindsight from the vantage of post-resurrection faith in him). The soteriological aspect of Jesus' whole life and ministry was already part of the pre-Pauline kerygma (1 Cor 15:3 ["Christ died for our sins"—note the same preposition "for," *hyper*]; Rom 4:25 ["he was handed over (to death) for our trespasses and raised for our justification"]; 1 Thess 1:10). Whether or not we can answer the historical question about what formula Jesus actually used at the "last supper," the New Testament references to the institution of the eucharist by him on that occasion have, in one form or another, associated such a soteriological connotation with it.

    i. The perennial question emerges about the extent to which these words of Jesus reflect an awareness of his own destiny and of the giving of his life vicariously as a sacrifice for others. The discussion in the preceding section reveals an answer to that question in the sense that in the early Christian community his words were already so *understood.* Against the background of Exodus 24:3–8 (the sacrificial ratification of the covenant of Sinai with the use of blood), the reference to the "blood of the covenant," present in some way in each formula used over the cup of wine, enhances the identification of the wine with Jesus' blood with the added sacrificial connotation. This much of an interpretive meaning may be traced back to Jesus himself, in some form. But these words reveal how difficult it is to separate the intention of his "very words" (*ipsissima verba*) from the interpreted intention of the subsequent tradition or of the evangelist's redaction. There is no solid reason to think that a soteriological, vicarious intention is not to be traced to what Jesus said over the bread and the wine at the "last supper." But there is simply no way of being certain about what went on in the mind of the Jesus of history on that occasion as he faced the prospect of death. We should all love to be able to answer such a question definitively; but who can, apart from a definitive intervention of the magisterium? (However, this is precisely the type of question in which the magisterium has not yet intervened and is unlikely ever to do so.)

Here once again it is important to realize that the twentieth century Christian's faith in the eucharist does not depend on what he or she can reconstruct of the words of the historical Jesus, but rather on the words as reflected to us through the early Christian community that recorded its diverse, varied recollections of him and of his impact on them in this matter. See §17h below.

j. In some of the New Testament accounts the early church has passed on to us a tradition about Jesus' expectation that his followers were to reenact the "last supper" as a rite among themselves, in memory of him (recall the memento-directive of 1 Cor 11:24–25; Lk 22:19c). Nothing is said, however, of this expectation in the Marcan or Matthean passages. The church's eventual understanding of that rite as "sacramental" is rooted in what Jesus did and said at the "last supper." But none of the New Testament texts depict him associating this specific sacramental understanding with his words or actions. Rather, it took time for the Christian community to come to an awareness of this aspect of what he had done.

Similarly, the Pauline passage, being restricted to a brief recital of the essentials (in view of the argument which Paul was making), says nothing about who was at table with Jesus "on the night he was betrayed." The synoptic narratives, however, provide some details about the occasion. The Marcan account portrays Jesus eating the "last supper" with the twelve (14:17); the Matthean account is similar ("with the twelve disciples," 26:20). Luke also tells us of his sitting at table with "the apostles" (22:14), the name given to the twelve in Luke 6:13 (but cf. 22:39). The memento-directive, recorded in the Pauline and Lucan accounts, would have been directed, then, to these select disciples. But in what sense? To them only? Or to them as representatives of all Jesus' followers? Was the supper to be reenacted only during the lifetime of the twelve, or even after them? We can answer the last question by arguing from what Paul says when he speaks of the eucharistic rite as a way of proclaiming the Lord's death "until he comes" (1 Cor 11:26). Those Pauline words, which scarcely envisage an imminent parousia, see the eucharistic rite as a way of proclaiming the soteriological death of Jesus the risen Lord. Those words imply that the reenactment of the "last supper" was not to be limited to the first generation of Christian disciples. Their successors were to continue it too. But who among them was to reenact it? There is no way of telling from what we have inherited from the early church's retelling of the "last supper" what might have been Jesus' intention in this regard. See further R.E. Brown, *Priest and Bishop: Biblical Reflections* (New York/Paramus, NJ: Paulist, 1970) 40–45. Thus the New Testament data regarding the "last supper" leave far more things open than most twentieth century Christians would suspect.

16.　Who Was Responsible for the Death of Jesus?

Literary evidence and new archaeological discoveries have often been invoked in recent times to serve as a background for the interpretation of the gospel accounts about the interrogation and trial of Jesus of Nazareth. Passages in the writings of Josephus, of the Qumran sect, of rabbinic literature, and even of the apocryphal gospels have been used along with inscriptions and older material from Roman historians to shed some light on the gospel accounts themselves. But no combination of this material has yet yielded a satisfying answer to the question about the responsibility for the death of Jesus.

a. The New Testament itself, which is the primary source of information about his interrogation, trial, and death, points an accusing finger at both Roman authority and Jewish leadership in Palestine of the time. It makes this accusation, however, with varying degrees of emphasis, depending on the individual New Testament writers. Modern Christians tend not to notice this variance of emphasis, but it has to be stressed.

b. The most extreme accusation is found in the earliest writing of the New Testament, in Paul's first letter to the Thessalonians. There he speaks of "the Jews" (without any distinction) "who killed the Lord Jesus" (2:14–15); no mention is made of the Romans. This passage has often been regarded as the most anti-semitic (in the modern sense of the adjective) in the Christian Bible.

c. In the passion narratives of the gospels one can detect a tendency to inculpate the Jewish leaders and to exculpate the Roman prefect, Pontius Pilate. This tendency becomes evident, not in any one gospel itself, but as the gospel tradition grows and as one compares the treatment of the two parties in the four gospels. Thus, in the earliest passion narrative, the responsibility is shared by chief priests, elders, and scribes of the Jewish people (Mk 14:1, 43, 53, 55; 15:1, 11) and by Pilate (15:15, "wishing to satisfy the crowd").

d. In the Matthean passion narrative the presentation differs little from the Marcan details (see 26:3, 47, 57, 59; 27:1, 20). This is because the Matthean passion narrative follows the Marcan closely. But there are peculiarly Matthean additions that clearly modify the picture of Pilate's role: (1) his wife warns him to have nothing to do "with that innocent man" (27:19); (2) Pilate washes his hands and declares openly his non-involvement: "I am innocent of the blood of this man; see to it yourselves. And all the people answered, 'His blood be upon us and upon our children' " (27:24–25).

e. In the Lucan passion narrative, which depends on the Marcan but is independent of the Matthean, the tendency is continued, but in a different way. Luke takes pains to distinguish at first "the people" or "the crowd" (22:2; 23:27, 35a, 48) from "the leaders" or the "elders, chief priests, and scribes" (22:2, 52, 54; 23:1, 4, 13, 35b, 51). Moreover, he omits all reference to false witnesses or to accusations about the destruction of the temple, presenting Jesus rather as accused by the leaders solely of political agitation (23:2, 5, 18–19). Pilate is here depicted declaring Jesus innocent three times over (23:4, 14–15, 22). When Pilate finally gives in, Luke makes it clear that "their voices prevailed; so Pilate gave sentence that their demand [for Barabbas] be granted . . . but Jesus he delivered to *their will*" (23:23–25). Verse 26 continues, "And as they led him away [to crucifixion]. . . ." Here the "they" can refer only to the immediately preceding "their" (v. 25) or to the remote "chief priests and rulers of the people" (v. 13). It is only at v. 36 that (Roman) soldiers appear! And they mock Jesus as "the king of the Jews."

   f. Finally, in the Johannine gospel what was emerging in the Lucan passion narrative comes to even clearer expression. The council of chief priests and Pharisees gather against Jesus and discuss his effect on the people and the likely reaction of the Romans (11:47–53); Caiaphas is made to say, "It is expedient that one man should die for the people and that the whole nation should not perish" (v. 50). Then soldiers and officers from the chief priests and Pharisees deal with Judas (18:3, 12–14 [here, however, some commentators try to see a reference to Romans in vv. 3, 12; see R.E. Brown, *Gospel according to John XIII–XXI* (AB 29A; Garden City, NY: Doubleday, 1970) 807–13]; the Johannine tradition is here at least ambiguous). When Jesus is finally brought before Pilate, he is again declared to be innocent three times over by the prefect (18:38; 19:4, 6), who seeks to free him (18:31; 19:12). But when Pilate finally yields, the evangelist records, "Then he handed him over to them to be crucified" (19:16), where "them" in the context can refer only to "the chief priests" of v. 15. Verse 17 continues, "So they took Jesus; and he went out, bearing his own cross."

   g. This comparison of details about the involvement of Pilate and Jewish leaders in the canonical passion narratives reveals a tendency at work in these writings that gradually makes the Jewish leaders more and more responsible for the death of Jesus. This tendency is carried forward in apocryphal writings such as the *Gospel of Peter,* where Pilate, seeing that none of the Jews, "neither Herod nor any of his judges would agree to wash their hands," as he had symbolically done, walks out on them. "Then Herod the king commanded that the Lord should be marched off" (§1–2; see *HSNTA,* 1. 183). And when Joseph of Arimathea later asks Pilate for Jesus' body, Pilate has to beg for it from Herod (§3–5). Thus Pilate gradually becomes "the good guy," and the "Jewish" king Herod is depicted as making the decision about Jesus' death and burial.

It is generally recognized that the tendency thus detected in the canonical passion narratives and the apocryphal *Gospel of Peter* undoubtedly reflects an attitude of early Christians who lived in various parts of the Roman empire and had to achieve recognition in it and seek for a *modus vivendi* within it. Christianity sought to be acknowledged in the empire as a *religio licita* (to borrow a term of later vintage), and this meant defining its relationship toward both Judaism (already so recognized) and the empire. No one can document this attitude or even the effort to play down Pilate's own involvement in the death of Jesus more precisely from other evidence than what we have presented here. Yet the tendency mentioned led in time to the notorious patristic and medieval charges of deicide leveled against the Jewish people. To cite but two examples: "Therefore the blood of Jesus came not only upon those who then lived, but upon all generations of Jews who followed thereafter even to the end (of the world)" (Origen, *Comm. in Matt.* ser. 124; PG 13. 1775); "And therefore the Jews sinned, not only as crucifiers of the man Christ, but also of God" (Thomas Aquinas, *S.T.* 3.47,5). This tendency, of course, complicates the attempt to answer the question originally posed.

i. In modern times attempts have been made to compare the details in the passion narratives with regulations in the Mishnah, the nucleus and earliest part of the rabbinic writings. Its sixty-three tractates, quoting the sayings of the fathers, i.e. the rabbis of various generations, were compiled under R. Judah the Prince at the beginning of the third century A.D. and reduced to writing. The tractate *Sanhedrin* contains various regulations about capital punishment and lawsuits dealing with it (e.g. 4:1; see H. Danby, *The Mishnah* [Oxford: Oxford University, 1933] 386–87). Attempts have been made to show that the interrogation of Jesus by Jewish leaders as portrayed in the gospels could never have taken place as recorded, or that the interrogation violates the regulations for due juridical process in the Jewish Mishnah. Such comparison, however, leads nowhere, since neither set of writings, neither the Christian gospels nor the Jewish traditions compiled in the Mishnah in post-New Testament times, can be taken as historical documents of the sort that would permit a competent judgment or a valid answer to be given to the question posed. The discrepancies between the synoptic accounts of the interrogation (one or two? at night or in the morning?) cannot be minimized. But it is equally impossible to establish that the idyllic regulations for judicial procedure recorded in the tractate *Sanhedrin* were actually in vogue in pre-70 Palestine. Both the Mishnah and the gospels are religious writings, composed for purposes other than answering historical questions such as the one posed.

j. The *Acts of Pilate* (*HSNTA*, 1. 444–70), which purports to be an account of Jesus' trial sent by the prefect to the emperor Tiberius in Rome, is manifestly a Christian composition of later date; it is devoid of any reliability as an independent historical testimony.

k. In recent times the thesis has often been proposed that only the Romans were responsible for the death of Jesus. It has been claimed that Palestinian Jewish authorities did not crucify or were incompetent to execute criminals, given the Roman occupation of the country at that time and the reservation of capital punishment to the occupiers (see Jn 18:31). There is, indeed, reason to acknowledge that the power of execution under the Romans was restricted. But it is far from clear that crucifixion was never employed by Jews

Jesus could crucify N13

in Palestine. The Hasmonean king Alexander Janneus (103–76 B.C.) crucified eight hundred of his enemy Jews (Josephus, *Ant.* 13.14,2 §380; *J.W.* 1.4,5–6 §93–98), and the recently published Temple Scroll from Qumran Cave 11 speaks clearly of crimes that call for such punishment (see 11QTemple 64:13; cf. my article, "Crucifixion in Ancient Palestine, Qumran Literature, and the New Testament," *CBQ* 40 [1978] 493–513, esp. pp. 503–04).

As a result, we cannot prove that some Jewish leaders of occupied Palestine or that Pilate and the Romans were *solely* responsible for the death of Jesus. Yet there is no real evidence to show that the general picture of the canonical passion narratives, which implicates both parties, is wholly untrustworthy.

✓ 17. Are There Different Interpretations of Jesus as the Christ (or Different Christologies) in the New Testament?

There are, indeed, and the sooner that readers of the New Testament learn to respect them, the better their comprehension of the New Testament will become. The tendency in the past to harmonize the data has been the cause of much misunderstanding about Jesus and his status as the God-man.

As already intimated (see §10d above), the "christology" of Jesus' earthly ministry can only be considered implicit or indirect. He sowed seeds during his ministry for what came to be recognized about him. What we call a "christology" today—the abstract term goes beyond the New Testament—is the product of a reflex mode of thought that synthesizes and makes explicit what New Testament writers had only partly formulated. Indeed, the affirmations about Jesus may have already made more explicit what was only implicit in his words, conduct, and teaching. But the "christology" of Paul, Luke, or John is a modern synthesis of what these New Testament writers have often left only concretely stated. To put it another way, one has to learn to respect the differences among the Pauline Christ Jesus, the Lucan Lord and savior, and the Johannine Word-made-flesh.

It is impossible to spell out here all the details of the different New Testament christologies, but a few broad strokes may highlight some of the nuances that are to be respected.

a. Some New Testament books have relatively little christology. For example, the epistle of James mentions "the Lord Jesus Christ" only two times, once in the opening address of the letter (1:1) to identify the supposed author, and once to mention him in whom one is to put one's faith (2:1). Apart from the title "Lord," there is scarcely an affirmation about who he really is for the author.

b. In Paul's letters, the earliest New Testament writings, we find little that could be considered constitutive or ontological christology, because Paul is more interested in interpreting the significance of Christ Jesus *for* human beings than in telling us what Jesus was, what he did, or what he said.

Paul hints at the pre-existence of Christ by adopting a primitive Christian hymn and making it part of an exhortation in Philippians 2:6–11. He speaks, moreover, of Christ as God's "Son" (Rom 1:3; 8:32) and even suggests something about his ontological relationship to "God the Father," precisely as "the Son himself" in 1 Corinthians 15:24–28. This passage cannot be understood solely in a functional way, because in it the Son's role and relation to humanity and all creation is presumed to have come to an end: "Then comes the end, when he delivers the kingdom to God the Father after destroying every rule and every authority and power. . . . When all things are subjected to him, then the Son himself will also be subjected to him who put all things under him, that God may be everything to everyone" (vv. 24, 28). Christ's salvific role will have been terminated, and in its termination he will still be recognized in his essential relation as Son of the Father.

Paul uses, indeed, explicit christological titles (e.g., Lord, Son of God, Messiah), but he is really far more interested in soteriology than in christology as such. His letters are replete with modes of describing the effects of the Christ-event, what Christ Jesus has done for humanity in his ministry, passion, death, burial, resurrection, exaltation, and heavenly intercession. When Paul looks back at that complex, he attributes to it a "once-for-all" character (*ephapax,* Rom 6:10); he sees it under various images reflecting not only his own Jewish and Hellenistic backgrounds, but also the controversies and debates of his missionary experience.

He sees the effect of that complex at times as "justification" (Gal 2:16–21; Rom 3:21–26; 4:25), "salvation" (Rom 1:16; 5:9; 10:10), "reconciliation" (2 Cor 5:18–20; Rom 5:10–11; 11:15), "redemption/ransom" (Rom 3:24; 8:23), "freedom" (Gal 5:1, 13; 2 Cor 3:17; Rom 8:2), "transformation/metamorphosis" (2 Cor 3:16–18; Rom 12:2), "new creation" (Gal 6:15; 2 Cor 5:17), "expiation" (Rom 3:25), "new life" (1 Cor 15:45; Rom 6:4), "adoptive sonship" (Gal 4:4–6; Rom 8:14–16), "sanctification" (1 Cor 1:30; 6:11), and possibly "forgiveness/pardon" of sins (Rom 3:25 [*paresis,* of disputed meaning]; Col 1:14 and Eph 1:7 [of disputed Pauline authorship]). Only Johannine soteriology and christology, distinctive with its own emphases, can come near to the richness of the Pauline view of Christ Jesus.

c. Lucan christology includes neither incarnation nor preexistence; these notions are not found in either the third gospel or Acts. It knows of Jesus' exaltation/ascension, but is silent about his heavenly intercession. It makes abundant use of early explicit titles (messiah, Lord, savior, Son, prophet, servant, Son of Man, teacher), but also has some which are exclusively Lucan: suffering messiah (Lk 24:26, 46; Acts 3:18; 17:3; 26:23), author of life (Acts 3:15; 5:31), messiah designate (Acts 3:20), and holy and righteous one (Acts 3:14). Luke too has a way of looking back at the effects of the Christ-event, but in contrast to the multiple images employed by Paul, he sums up his soteriology only under a few figures: "salvation" (Lk 2:30; Acts 13:26; alone among the synoptic evangelists, Luke calls Jesus "savior," 2:11; cf. Acts 5:31; 13:23); "forgiveness of

sins" (*aphesis,* Lk 24:47; Acts 13:38), "peace" (Lk 2:14; 19:42; Acts
10:36), and "justification" (Acts 13:39 [but with a nuance different
from the Pauline understanding of it]).

    d. Johannine christology, however, moves with a much deeper
understanding of explicit christology. It insists on understanding
Jesus as one in whom God is seen among human beings and in
whom God's salvation is now concretized in a totally new way. Jesus
in his person replaces the presence of God-among-men of old (the
shekināh-idea) and the institutions of Judaism (the temple, the ritual washings, the manna as the bread of life). Johannine christology
is "high," including the incarnation of the Word, the identification
of the Son with the Father in their concern for the world, and even
elements of a relational, ontological christology (the Word was not
only with God, but was God, 1:1). It is to be noted that the Jesus of
the Johannine gospel, all during his earthly ministry, speaks as if he
were already in glory; because of this, the Johannine Jesus makes
such statements as "Before Abraham was, I am" (8:58); "I and the
Father are one" (10:30). These statements, put on Jesus' lips by the
fourth evangelist, are precisely the building blocks of the "high"
christology that one meets in the Johannine writings and that make
it so different from that of other New Testament writings.

    This christology, however, co-exists along with a number of
explicit titles derived from the earlier tradition: messiah (even explained as "Christ," 1:41), Son of God (1:34), teacher (1:38, as a
translation of "rabbi"), king of Israel (12:13), Son of Man (1:51;
3:13, etc.), prophet (4:19), Savior (4:42 [shared with Luke]). But it
also has a number of its own titles: "Lamb of God" (1:29, 36); "good
shepherd" (10:11); "bread of life" (6:35, 51). These exclusively Johannine titles are more expressive of soteriology than of christology.
The effects of the Christ-event in the Johannine view are set forth
under the following figures: "salvation" (3:17; 12:47), "taking away
of sin" (1:29), "enlightenment" (1:9), "empowering" human beings
"to become children of God" (1:12; 3:5–7), giving a "share in eter-

nal life" (3:36; 4:14; 5:24), precisely through the "resurrection" (11:25–26).

e. Another whole area in which one would have to distinguish New Testament christologies is that of the relation of Jesus to the Spirit. Whereas Paul does not always clearly distinguish the risen Christ from the Spirit (e.g. 2 Cor 3:17: "The Lord is the Spirit"; cf. 1 Cor 15:45; Rom 1:4), there are triadic passages in his letters where the parallelism implies a distinction (such as 1 Cor 12:4–6; 2 Cor 13:14). The distinction, however, is made clear in both Lucan and Johannine christology (Lk 24:49; Acts 1:4; 2:4–21, 33; Jn 7:39; 14:26; 15:26; 16:7–11).

f. As we have sketched here briefly the Pauline, Lucan, and Johannine christologies, we could also do the same for the gospel according to Matthew, the epistle to the Hebrews, and the book of Revelation, three important New Testament writings, which have christologies of their own.

g. These differing christologies also reveal why it is difficult to write a theology of the New Testament in the way that one used to attempt it. For if there are differing christologies, there are also differing theologies in the New Testament. They cannot be simply harmonized, and that is why it is wrong to interpret passages in the gospels by Pauline ideas or sayings of Jesus in the synoptics by nuances from the Johannine tradition. The different christologies in the New Testament amount to different portraits of Jesus that the early Christian community has sketched of him and left behind as its heritage to feed the faith of subsequent generations and centuries of Christian believers.

h. If our answers to questions 1 and 2 above were somewhat negative and minimal, it is good to remember that the faith of modern Christians is not measured by what they can establish historically about Jesus of Nazareth. Faith in the twentieth century means an allegiance to him who entered human history as God's agent and Son, but also to him as reflected and refracted in the experience and *an ideal approach!*

tradition of the early Christian community. This is not to put a book (the New Testament) between Jesus and the modern believer, or even the christologies of the early Christians between them. However, the inspired christologies are normative of Christian faith, in a way in which none of the later tradition is. The twentieth century Christian has no pipeline to Jesus apart from or independent of these writings and these christologies, different as they are. Two things have to be kept in tandem, Jesus of Nazareth *and* the early Christian portraits of him. These are the *norma normans* of all later christological and soteriological teaching. This will be further developed as we proceed.

18. How Are References to the Resurrection of Jesus in the New Testament To Be Interpreted?

The resurrection of Jesus is the cardinal affirmation of Christian faith found in the New Testament and passed on to us by early Christians. To confess that "Jesus is Lord," one has to admit that "God raised him from the dead" (Rom 10:9) and that "if Christ has not been raised, then is our preaching in vain and your faith is vain too" (1 Cor 15:14). Not to admit the resurrection of Jesus means that one is not a Christian.

a. The problem which modern readers of the New Testament have with the resurrection of Jesus is not so much the basic Christian kerygma (enshrined in such passages as 1 Cor 15:3–7; 1 Thess 1:9–10; Rom 4:25) as with (1) either the resurrection narratives of the gospel tradition or (2) the way in which they tend to imagine to themselves what the New Testament has to say about the risen Christ.

b. First of all, one has to reckon with six different resurrection narratives in the New Testament:

(1) *Mark 16:1–8,* which is the conclusion of the Marcan gospel in the best Greek manuscripts of that gospel (Vaticanus, Sinaticus).

(Three other endings are found in some manuscripts: [i] the canonical appendix to the Marcan gospel, vv. 9–20, found in the Koine text-tradition and codices A, C, D, W, L, etc. [see 6 below]; [ii] an expanded v. 8 in codices L, 099, 0112, etc.; and [iii] the so-called Freer Logion, added to v. 14 in codex Washingtonianus. These have been secondarily added to supply the Marcan gospel with accounts of the appearances of the risen Christ, as in other gospels.) Verses 1–8, however, report only the discovery of the empty tomb by the women, Mary Magdalene, Mary the mother of James, and Salome, the *praeconium paschale,* "the Easter proclamation," that "he has been raised; he is not here" (v. 6c), and the silence and withdrawal of the women, "for they were afraid" (*ephobounto gar,* with a conjunction forming the strange ending of a biblical book!). These Marcan verses have no description of the resurrection itself nor any appearances of the risen Christ, but they do promise that Peter and others will see him in Galilee.

(2) *Matthew 28:1–20,* which likewise reports the discovery of the empty tomb and the Easter message, "He is not here, for he has been raised, as he said" (vv. 1–8). But this narrative includes an appearance of the risen Christ in Jerusalem to Mary Magdalene and the other Mary (vv. 9–10), the report and bribery of the guard by the chief priests and elders (vv. 11–15), another appearance of Christ to the eleven in Galilee (vv. 16–17), and his commission to them to make other disciples by teaching and baptism (vv. 18–20).

(3) *Luke 24:1–53,* which also tells of the finding of the empty tomb and of the Easter message, "He is not here, but has been raised" (vv. 1–12), but also of appearances of the risen Christ on the road to Emmaus (vv. 13–35) and in Jerusalem (vv. 36–43), of his commission to his disciples to be "witnesses of these things" (vv. 44–49), and of his ascension on the evening of the day of the discovery of the empty tomb (vv. 50–53).

(4) *John 20:1–29,* which records the finding of the empty tomb (vv. 1–10) and recounts the appearance of the risen Christ to Mary Magdalene (vv. 11–18), to disciples in Jerusalem (with Thomas, one

of the twelve, absent, vv. 19–23), and again to disciples (with Thomas present, vv. 24–29).

(5) *The Johannine appendix (21:1–23),* which resumes the narrative after the concluding verses of 20:30–31 and tells only of Christ's appearance to seven disciples in Galilee (with the contrasting roles of Peter and the beloved disciple set forth).

(6) *The appendix to the Marcan gospel (16:9–20),* which is found only in some Greek manuscripts (see above) and reports three appearances of Jesus in Jerusalem or its environs on Easter Sunday (vv. 9–11, 12–13, 14–18) and his "being taken up" on the evening of that same day.

c. In contrast to the notable parallelism among the four passion narratives, the resurrection narratives go their own ways, save for the four accounts of the discovery of the empty tomb and two verses in the Marcan appendix (16:12–13), which may refer to the Emmaus incident (Lk 24:13–35). This diversity of the appearance stories is puzzling: Why should there not have been more agreement among them, or at least agreement of them with the list of witnesses recorded in 1 Corinthians 15:5–7? Even the "great commission," present in Matthew 28:18–20; Luke 24:47–49; Mark 16:15–16, is in each gospel actually suited to the theological thrust of that writing (even in the appendix of the Marcan gospel).

Moreover, the stories of Jesus' appearances are sometimes "concise" (to use C.H. Dodd's form-critical terminology), i.e. well-rounded and shaped by frequent repetition (e.g. Mt 28:8–10, 16–20; Jn 20:19–23); sometimes they are dramatic or "circumstantial" tales (e.g. Lk 24:13–35; Jn 21:1–14), where the creative hand of the evangelist has been at work, fashioning details and conversations and observing the unities of time and space; and sometimes they are "mixed," i.e. concise stories on the way to becoming "circumstantial" tales (e.g. Mk 16:14–15; Lk 24:36–43; Jn 20:11–18, 24–29). In other words, the accounts of Jesus' appearances are the products of varying traditions and composition and are scarcely reflections of the earliest level of preaching about the risen Christ.

By contrast, the earliest levels of the New Testament tradition speak at times of Jesus' "exaltation" to glory from his death on the cross, omitting all reference to the resurrection (see the pre-Pauline Christian hymn used in Phil 2:8–11; cf. 1 Tim 3:16, also a primitive piece used in a later writing). The resurrection narratives, with all their diversity, have to be seen as attempts to fill out the details of the reports of appearances of the risen Christ preserved in such a fundamental proclamation as 1 Corinthians 15:3–7.

d. Was the tomb really found empty? This is not merely a modern question, since the Matthean gospel reflects a Christian reaction to objections about it or to a question of this sort: 27:62–66 (the sealing of the tomb and the posting of the guard); 28:11–15 (the report of the guard and the bribing of them). These passages are peculiar to Matthew and bear the obvious marks of apologetics against "the Jews." But they are confined to one gospel and scarcely account for every form of the story of the empty tomb (e.g. in the earlier Marcan narrative, or in the almost certainly independent Johannine tradition).

In the 1930s a first-century ossuary turned up in Jerusalem bearing the name of the deceased, *Yēshûa' bar Yehôsēph,* "Jesus son of Joseph." (An ossuary is a stone box used for the "second burial" of the collected bones of a dead person after the flesh has decomposed.) The Jewish scholar who discovered the ossuary and published the inscription, E.L. Sukenik (the father of Y. Yadin, the former deputy prime minister of Israel), drew no conclusions from it about any New Testament personage, realizing that "Jesus" and "Joseph" were commonly used names for Palestinian Jews in the first century. Such a discovery scarcely invalidated the story of the empty tomb.

It is sometimes argued, however, that Paul in the kerygmatic fragment used in 1 Corinthians 15:3–5 makes no mention of an empty tomb: "that Christ died for our sins according to the scriptures, that he was buried, that he was raised on the third day according to the scriptures, and that he appeared to Cephas, then to the

twelve. . . ." Hence the story of the empty tomb might seem to be of
later (apologetic) origin. True, the empty tomb is not mentioned in
this kerygmatic passage, but one has to reckon here with the parallel
four-item formulation of the first part of this fragment (death,
burial, resurrection, appearances), each introduced by *hoti,* "that."
The four items can also be found reflected in Paul's speech in Acts
13:28–31. Hence its formulaic character was clearly of greater kerygmatic value than the inclusion of all details. It may be that narrative accounts of the discovery of the empty tomb only came to be
formulated later than the kerygma itself, but this later emergence
does not really exclude all factuality itself, especially since the account of the discovery of the empty tomb was already part of the
primitive Marcan passion narrative (16:3–6) and was recorded also
in the independent Johannine gospel.

    e. The other modern problem with the resurrection of Jesus is
the way in which people tend to picture to themselves what the New
Testament has passed on about the risen Christ. Here several important points should be recalled:

    (1) Despite Acts 1:22, in the episode about the selection of
Matthias, which lists as a criterion for membership in the twelve one
who had been "a witness to the resurrection," *no one is said to have
witnessed the resurrection of Jesus.* It is never so put, not even in
Matthew 28:2b, which mentions the earthquake and the angel of the
Lord who descended, rolled back the stone of the tomb, and sat
upon it. In Acts 1:22 Luke has formulated abstractly what was really
meant: "a witness to the risen Christ" was to be the replacement of
Judas, i.e. one to whom Christ had appeared (similarly for Acts
4:33). For none of the canonical gospels attempts to do what the
later apocryphal *Gospel of Peter* does (§35–42):

> Now in the night in which the Lord's day dawned, when
> the soldiers were keeping guard, two by two in every watch,
> there rang out a loud voice in heaven. They saw the
> heavens opened, and two men came down from there in

great brightness and drew near to the sepulchre. That stone
which had been laid against the entrance to the sepulchre
started to roll of itself and gave way to the side, and the
sepulchre was opened, and both the young men entered in.
When then these soldiers saw this, they woke up the centurion and the elders, for they were also there to assist at
the watch. And while they were relating what they had
seen, they again saw three men come out of the sepulchre,
and two of them sustaining the other, and a cross following
them. They saw the heads of the two reaching to heaven,
but that of him who was led by them by the hand surpass-
ing the heavens. Then they heard a voice crying out of the
heavens, "Hast thou preached to them that sleep?" And
from the cross there was heard the answer, "Yes." (Cf.
HSNTA, 1. 185–86.)

Thus this apocryphal gospel imaginatively fills in the details of the
resurrection and describes the coming forth of Jesus from the tomb.
It represents an effort to answer later queries about how it happened,
or describes the resurrection, as Luke does the ascension in
Acts 1:9–11.

(2) The New Testament never presents the resurrection of
Jesus as a resuscitation or a reanimation, i.e. a return to his former
mode of terrestrial existence (like that, say, of Lazarus, Jn 11:43–44;
12:1–2). Jesus is never portrayed inhabiting the earth for forty days
or appearing as someone who had been ensconced behind an arras.
Indeed, Luke 24:37–39 strives explicitly to reject the idea that he
was like a spook.

(3) Though the New Testament does not say so explicitly, it
implies time and again that when the risen Christ appeared, he appeared from glory, i.e. from the glorious presence of the Father.
Romans 6:4 says that "Christ was raised from the dead by the glory
of the Father." And the risen Christ asks the disciples on the road to
Emmaus, "Did not the Christ have to suffer these things and *enter*

into his glory?" (Lk 24:26). Note the past tense "Was it not necessary that . . ." used by the risen Christ on the day itself of the discovery of the empty tomb. Moreover, the only difference between the
appearance of the risen Christ to Paul on the road to Damascus and
that to the others earlier was, in reality, a temporal one, i.e. it happened to Paul in the Lucan account after the events of Pentecost.
This has to be recognized despite the Lucan differences of descrip-
tive details. The "spatial" *terminus a quo* of the appearances should
not be understood as different in these cases.

(4) Whereas the risen Christ who appears to his disciples insists
on his identity, he is also said to have appeared "in another form"
(appendix to the Marcan gospel, 16:12). He was at first recognized
by neither Cleopas and his companion (Lk 24:16) nor Mary Magdalene (Jn 20:1–16). However one wants to explain this, one must
recall in this connection Paul's admission that there is a difference
between a "physical body" sown in death and a "spiritual body"
raised therefrom (1 Cor 15:42–44). Indeed, when Paul tries to describe the risen body, he identifies it expressly with what is not
"body," viz. "spirit(ual)." Are we to write that off simply as a rhetorical oxymoron? Scarcely. But it says something about how we should
envision the risen Christ and his "glorified" body.

f. The kerygma of early Christianity, which proclaimed the
death, burial, raising, and appearances of Christ, originated in a
Palestinian Jewish-Christian setting, wherein the notion of the afterlife was not that of the Greek philosophical dichotomy of body/soul
or the immortality of the soul. It arose in a milieu in which "resurrection" (see Dan 12:2) would only have been understood as a bodily
resurrection. Perhaps we cannot explain just what such a view of
afterlife would entail. But the early kerygma did not content itself to
affirm merely that Jesus was alive or that he was a living influence in
the lives of his followers. It included an admission that Jesus had
been "raised" to a state of glory in the presence of the Father, and
that would have had to mean "raised bodily."

Even though some biblical interpreters would like to dismiss the idea of a bodily resurrection of Jesus and are skeptical about the empty-tomb tradition, we must emphasize that the bodily resurrection of Jesus to glory is a basic part of the New Testament kerygmatic proclamation and a fundamental affirmation of Christian faith.

19. How Are New Testament References to the Ascension To Be Understood?

a. In analyzing the different references in the New Testament to Jesus' ascension, we must reckon with their varying nuances.

(1) The earliest references speak of Jesus' transit to the Father or to glory as an "exaltation" and use this term in a way that makes it difficult to be sure whether the resurrection or the ascension (or possibly both) is meant. These references seem to describe a passage from death on the cross to a heavenly existence with the Father in glory without mention of the resurrection (see Phil 2:8–11, part of the pre-Pauline hymn used there, and the primitive hymn embedded in 1 Tim 3:16; recall also the Johannine mode of speaking about Jesus being "lifted up," e.g. 12:32–34 [on the cross? or to glory?]).

(2) Some New Testament passages refer to the ascension without describing it or fixing it in time or place (e.g. Rom 10:6 [by implication]; more explicitly, Eph 4:8–10). In such passages, Christ's ascension is taken for granted and is used to make some other theological affirmation, e.g. the ease of Christian faith (Rom 10) or the bounty of the glorified Christ to the Christian community (Eph 4).

(3) Some New Testament passages refer to Jesus' being "carried up to heaven," being "taken up to heaven," or "ascending" to the Father on the day of the discovery of the empty tomb (Lk 24:51; the appendix to the Marcan gospel, 16:19; Jn 20:17). These passages fix a date (Easter Sunday) and a term (heaven, the Father) for this transit. They closely relate the ascension to the event of

Easter and thus differ only slightly from the mode of exaltation mentioned above in the first instance.

   (4) Acts 1:3, 9–11 gives a brief description of the transit and fixes it in time (some forty days after the resurrection [1:3]—but cf. Acts 13:31, simply "many days" [*hēmeras pleious*])—in space (from the Mount of Olives [1:12]), in a specific mode ("lifted up, with a cloud taking him out of sight" [1:9]), and in its term (heaven [1:11]). From this Lucan scene in Acts 1 we have inherited the traditional mode of representing to ourselves the "ascension." This scene is the only New Testament passage, however, which does this and does what the apocryphal *Gospel of Peter* sought to do for the resurrection (see §18e/1 above), i.e. depict Christ's coming out of the tomb. But Luke 24 has dated the "ascension" of Christ to Easter Sunday itself, in contrast to the date given in Acts 1. Scribes who later copied the codices Sinaiticus and Bezae and translator(s) of the *Vetus Latina* sought to solve the discrepancy by omitting the crucial words of Luke 24:51, "and he was carried up to heaven." In their critical edition of 1881, Westcott and Hort omitted these words and started a fad among New Testament textual critics. Since the discovery, however, of Papyrus Bodmer XIV, which is the oldest papyrus text of the Lucan gospel (dated A.D. 200 ± 25 years), textual critics no longer agree with their judgment. For those words are found not only in that oldest papyrus text, but also in the vast majority of the best Greek manuscripts. Moreover, they represent a reading which copyists would more logically have omitted (to solve the discrepancy) than added (to create one). Those words of v. 51, then, are the *lectio difficilior praeferenda* (the text-critical principle of preferring the more difficult reading). See P. Benoit, "The Ascension," *Jesus and the Gospel: Volume I* (New York: Herder and Herder, 1973) 209–53.

   b. "Ascent/ascension" means motion upward, and implied in the New Testament accounts of Jesus' ascension is a movement through the heavens or the celestial spheres (see Eph 4:10; cf. Aristotle, *Metaphys.* 12.8 1073a). The transit to "the Father" or "to God" (Jn 20:17) has at times employed in the New Testament not only apocalyptic stage-props ("being taken up to heaven," with "a cloud" as a vehicle) but also made use of a time-conditioned sense of "heaven(s)." There is, moreover, a fluctuation in the terminology, between a passive assumption ("he was taken/carried up" [by God/ the Father]) and an active ascension ("I am ascending" [Jn 20:17], "one who ascended" [Eph 4:8]). These time-conditioned elements and fluctuations create part of the difficulty in trying to understand what is really meant.

c. The "ascension" affirms for the Christian readers of the New Testament that the risen, exalted Christ is with the Father in glory (recall Lk 24:26), whence he sends the Spirit to his followers as a dynamic and effective mode of his presence among them, when he is no longer visibly manifest to them.

What is really at issue in the New Testament passages dealing with the "ascension" of Jesus is an attempt to describe the complex phase of his existence that we variously refer to as his resurrection, exaltation, ascension, or transit to the Father, along with his continued presence to his followers/church in his life-giving Spirit. This complex, including his death, is, in the proper sense, the "paschal mystery."

Once we realize that Jesus' resurrection has not been presented in the New Testament as a resuscitation or a return to terrestrial life or existence, but as a bodily resurrection to the glorious presence of the Father, and that his appearances to his disciples were made from that glory, then his "ascension" is readily understood as his final appearance, as his visible leave-taking from his assembled followers. He would no longer so present himself to them in their corporate unity (not yet called "church" in Acts). Henceforth, his "presence" among them would be through the Spirit, the "promise of my Father" (Lk 24:49; Acts 1:4), which he as one exalted to the right hand of God pours out (Acts 2:33). (He would also be present to them "in the breaking of the bread," as the Emmaus incident implies [Lk 24:35].) True, the risen Christ does present himself later to Saul of Tarsus on the road to Damascus, in a post-Pentecostal appearance (Acts 9:5; 22:8, 26:15), where Luke recounts once in dramatic form and twice in speeches what Paul himself refers to in 1 Corinthians 9:1 and Galatians 1:16 (without any reference to Pentecost). But that was an appearance of the risen Christ to an *individual,* a "vessel of election" (Acts 9:15), especially chosen to become "the apostle of the Gentiles" (Rom 11:13).

d. Related to the "ascension" is the gift of the Spirit, as the last paragraph implies. In Acts 2:4 the Spirit is "poured out" on Pentecost, fifty days after Passover (cf. 2:33). But in John 20:22 the Spirit is given by the risen Christ to the assembled disciples on the night of the day of the discovery of the empty tomb: "He breathed on them and said, 'Receive [the] Holy Spirit.' " This discrepancy of date about the giving of the Spirit to Christian disciples is similar to that of the "date" of the ascension, although in this case it is not a discrepancy found within the writings of the same New Testament author. We cannot resolve the question about when the Spirit was first bestowed upon early Christians, any more than we can date the "ascension." In either tradition (Lucan or Johannine) the basic affirmation of the gift is common: a bestowal which Paul, the earliest theologian of the New Testament, either affirms or takes for granted over and over again (Gal 3:2, 5; 4:6; Rom 8:2–3, 12–17; 1 Cor 12:3).

It is Luke who, in his well-known concern to press home the *reality* of the risen Christ and of the Spirit in Christian life, has historicized *phases* of the complex Christ-event and its effects. Facets of it have been dramatized to stress the reality of the gift and the reality of the presence and influence of the risen Christ. (See further my article, "The Ascension of Christ and Pentecost," *TS* 45 [1984] 409–40.)

20. Did Jesus Clearly Claim To Be God?

a. This question could be asked with different nuances. If it is meant as a query about the consciousness of the Jesus of history during his earthly ministry, it faces the problems already mentioned in §2e above. We have no way of answering what went on in his mind. The only documents that we have about what he did or said, which might reflect indirectly his awareness, were written at least a generation after his death. They scarcely reflect his direct or reflex consciousness in any explicit way.

The Johannine Jesus says, "I and the Father are one" (10:30) or "The Father is in me, and I am in the Father" (10:38). See further John 6:46; 8:58; 17:5. But can one appeal to such statements of the Johannine Jesus to answer the question posed in terms of his historical consciousness? One cannot ignore the Johannine context of such statements or the thrust of that gospel as a whole. To give this sort of answer to the question would be to give misguided reassurance to the "fundamentalism of the fearful" (to use a phrase of the Anglican bishop John A.T. Robinson, *Can We Trust the New Testament?* [Grand Rapids, MI: Eerdmans, 1977] 16). For even if one were to admit that Jesus did know and claim that he was divine, he would scarcely have formulated that claim in the mode of the statements of the Johannine gospel. For the articulation of that claim of the Johannine Jesus has resulted from a generation or more of meditation and speculative hindsight.

b. If the question is meant to stress a "clear claim," we can answer it in two ways:

(1) If the Jesus of history ever explicitly claimed to be God, the gospels have not so presented that claim. They never put on his lips *egō eimi theos,* "I am God."

True, New Testament writers attribute the title *theos* to him (e.g. Jn 1:1; 20:28; Heb 1:8). However, this is a "confessional" title, i.e. one that manifests a certain belief in him. It obviously corresponds to the period and experience of the Christianity that the writer represents. It is not a title that can with certainty be attributed to him in his earthly ministry. When it emerges in the New Testament tradition, it is found in the later canonical books.

(2) If the words "clearly claim" could be understood of an implication or impression conveyed by Jesus that he was a being who enjoyed a unique relationship to Yahweh or an "otherness" not shared by other human beings or even other heaven-sent emissaries, then one could give a guarded affirmative answer to the question. Various elements in the synoptic and Johannine traditions about him (see §10d above) convey the notion that what he passed on to others was at most an implicit and indirect impression of that relationship. It took time for the explication and unfolding of that relationship to be formulated and to be recorded in the New Testament itself: "and the Word was God" (Jn 1:1).

c. Two further comments must be made in this regard:

(1) One of the religious charges leveled against Jesus by his contemporaries and reflected in various ways in the New Testament is that of "blasphemy" (Mk 2:7; 14:64; Jn 10:33 ["being only a man, you make yourself God"], 36). This undoubtedly echoes an early Christian recollection of the main charge brought against him, even though the diversity of the contexts in which it now appears makes it almost impossible for us to specify the particulars of that charge. However, it is not unlikely that it was associated with an impression that Jesus had given about a unique relationship to Yahweh, that he was somehow on a par with Yahweh (see Jn 5:18).

(2) Would it have been possible in the monotheistic setting of pre-Christian Palestine for a Jew like Jesus to claim openly, *'anāh 'elāh* (in Aramaic) or *egō eimi theos* (in Greek), "I am God"? Indeed, to ask the question is to answer it. For it is impossible to imagine how such a statement would have been understood, given the fact that "God" would have meant the "one God" of Israel, Yahweh.

(Recall that in most instances in the New Testament *theos* is the Greek title used of Yahweh [of the one whom Jesus himself called *'abbā'*].)

d. Even if Jesus did not claim to be God, did he *know* that he was God? This would be simply another way of phrasing the question about the direct or reflex consciousness of Jesus of Nazareth? Yet for a Palestinian Jew of the first century "God" would have meant "Yahweh" or "the Father in heaven," and hence the question would have meant, "Did Jesus know that he was the Father in heaven?" Put that way, the answer would have to be no. For until Christian theologians had unpacked the meaning of "God," it would have been impossible to include the Son as well as the Father in heaven in such a designation. Yet Jesus had an intuitive knowledge of his self-identity, what we express in faith as being truly God and truly man. Whether he would have been able to conceptualize that intuition or formulate it in words to communicate it to others is another question, one that no one can answer. Certainly, Jesus of Nazareth would have been aware that he was not just another heaven-sent prophet.

e. In this regard it is important to recall that a New Testament writer calls Jesus "the firstborn of all creation" (Col 1:14), which eventually was interpreted by Arius to mean that there "was a time when the Word was not," i.e. that the Word was a creature. But the Council of Nicaea (A.D. 325) condemned that heretical contention (DS 130), and in its Creed acknowledged that the Word was *homoousios,* "one in being," with the Father (DS 125). Later in A.D. 451 the Council of Chalcedon taught that the same "Lord Jesus Christ . . . was truly God and truly man . . . consubstantial with the Father in divinity and consubstantial with us in humanity, (yet) one to be recognized (as existing) in two natures not confused, not changeably, not divided, but inseparably . . . and coming together in one person and subsistence" (DS 302). Thus both councils affirmed what had long been held about Jesus as the God-Man. This belief was based on a conviction that Jesus would have known who he was and shared that knowledge with his contemporaries in indirect ways, and that within a short time after his resurrection it would have given rise to the conviction that he was the Son of God and divine. Though the church has never defined that Jesus *knew* that he was God, its constant teaching about the pre-existence of the Word and of his incarnation must date from shortly after the resurrection itself: John's gospel (finally redacted ca. A.D. 90–95) is an eloquent testimony to such first century teaching. Implicit in such a teaching would be the conviction that Jesus knew that he was God.

   f. To confine ourselves to the New Testament data, however, we would have to say that Jesus of Nazareth was aware that he was related in a unique way to the God of Israel, Yahweh, whom he even addressed as *'abbā'* (Mk 14:36), and that he conveyed that awareness in some indirect way to his followers. Yet even this Jesus, when asked by the rich young man, "Good teacher, what must I do to inherit eternal life?" answers, "Why call me good? No one is good but God alone" (Mk 10:17–18; Lk 18:19). Here Jesus is portrayed asserting that a prerogative of God does not belong properly to him. Such a saying points up the problem about the awareness that Jesus had during his lifetime and ministry. Yet note how the answer that he gives to the young man is changed in the later gospel of Matthew: "What good deed must I do to have eternal life?" "Why do you ask me about what is good?" (19:16–17). Here one sees how a later evangelist was already coping with the problem of Jesus' implied divinity; his censorial red pencil prevented him from depicting Jesus denying the prerogative of divine goodness, as does the Marcan and Lucan Jesus.

   See further F.-P. Dreyfus, *Did Jesus Know He Was God?* (Chicago: Franciscan Herald, 1989), who answers the question affirmatively; but above all compare the more properly nuanced answer of R.E. Brown, "Did Jesus Know He Was God?" *BTB* 15 (1985) 74–79.

21. Did Jesus of Nazareth Know All Things, Even About the Future?

Again, this is a question seeking to psychoanalyze the Jesus of history, and it cannot be easily answered.

a. Luke 2:52 records that "Jesus advanced in wisdom, age, and favor before God and human beings." This implies that his knowledge was cumulative, and that in this regard he was like any other human being and was able to grow and develop intellectually. Hence, on the face of it, Jesus did not "know all things."

b. If one presses further and asks whether he *came to know* all things, there is no answer to that question in the New Testament. Yet it seems obvious that Jesus did not know all things in the future (e.g. the invention of printing or of the atomic or hydrogen bombs, the division of the Christian church, computer technology, the demise of communism). No one really expects that such knowledge of the future would have been his.

c. His knowledge of his own coming destiny (death by crucifixion) is also problematic. The synoptic gospels record a threefold prediction of his coming passion and death (Mk 8:31; 9:31; 10:33–34, and par.; other passages in the Lucan gospel could be added). Such passages suggest that Jesus did know what fate was in store for him. Yet when such passages are analyzed, these so-called predictions are seen to have been formulated with hindsight and include details drawn from the synoptic passion narratives. They cannot be simplistically regarded as actual predictions uttered by Jesus of Nazareth during his ministry. Yet there is no reason to question the substantial conviction that he undoubtedly had that he would die violently at the hands of his opponents. Though the classic threefold announcements prove to be stylistically formulated, they do not preclude that Jesus spoke to his disciples in a guarded fashion about a fate that might be his in Jerusalem. Whether he had any clear knowledge of the form of that fate (e.g. by stoning, or by crucifixion) is impossible to say, and is, in fact, unlikely. Note how Jesus is depicted speaking of his death in figurative language in Mark 10:38, "Can you drink of the cup that I drink or be baptized in the baptism with which I am baptized?"

d. Mark 13 and its synoptic parallels portray Jesus uttering an eschatological discourse, not only about the future of the Jerusalem temple, but also about coming days of tribulation. Yet even so Jesus in Mark 13:32 declares, "But of that day or that hour no one knows, not even the angels in heaven or the Son, but only the Father." Cf. Matthew 24:36.

e. The question is really asked from the standpoint of the definition of the Council of Chalcedon (A.D. 451), according to which Jesus was one divine person with two natures, human and divine. Consequently, he would have had not only a human intellect, but also a divine intellect. In that context, one can ask whether his human intellect, with its finite capacity, was aware of all that his divine intellect knew. If with his divine intellect he knew that he was God and knew all things, even the future, his human intellect hypostatically united to his divine nature would have had some limited, non-conceptual human understanding of such things. But the New Testament gives no inkling of the teaching of Chalcedon. That council not only reformulated in other language the New Testament data about Jesus' constitution, but also reconceptualized it in the light of the current Greek philosophical thinking. And that reconceptualization and reformulation go well beyond the New Testament data.

22. What Is To Be Said of the Titles Messiah or Christ, Son of Man, Son of God, Lord, etc.?

Such titles are important data in the New Testament for its explicit christological teaching about Jesus and his role in the divine plan of salvation. For the most part, they are titles born of Christian, post-resurrectional faith and represent confessional affirmations about him. Early Christians clearly used them, but the problem is to explain their emergence. Three questions have to be asked about them: (1) What is the origin or background of the title? (2) What did it mean? (3) To what phase of Jesus' existence was it initially applied? For some of them have been retrojected by hindsight from post-resurrection settings into stories of the ministry or infancy. Here it is impossible to discuss each of these aspects of the titles at length, but brief remarks on some of them will be attempted.

With the possible exception of "Son of Man," there is no evidence that the earthly Jesus ever used these titles of himself.

a. "Messiah" (or "Christ") is a title derived from the Old Testament and from pre-Christian Palestinian Judaism. It designates an anointed agent sent by God for the welfare or salvation of his people. Used in the Old Testament for historical kings who sat on David's throne, it assumed political connotations (see Pss 18:51; 89:39, 52; 132:10, 17), assuring the continuance of the Davidic dynasty. In the postexilic period, when the dynasty was no more, the title was used of the high priest (Lev 4:3, 5). When the messianic expectation clearly emerged in Judaism, the first mention of a *coming* messiah is found in Daniel 9:25 (final redaction of the book of Daniel, ca. 165 B.C.). Almost about the same time the Qumran community begins to speak of a "messiah of Israel" and a "messiah of Aaron" (1QS 9:11), and begins to predicate the title even of Israel's prophets.

As a title for Jesus in the New Testament, it is missing in the "Q" source of the synoptic tradition. In three places in the Marcan gospel it probably reflects the post-resurrectional concerns of the early Christian church (9:41; 13:21; 15:32). Whether three other Marcan passages that use it (8:29; 12:35; 14:61–62) are reflections of authentic usage coming from the ministry of Jesus is debated.

In the first of these, Mark 8:29, Peter's confession of Jesus as "the Christ" (or "messiah") forms the literary turning-point of Jesus' relation to his disciples and of the Marcan revelation of who Jesus is. Does it permit an historical deduction about Peter's recognition of Jesus during his ministry? It undoubtedly enshrines something of a Petrine recognition, which may have been sharpened in time in its messianic form (recall the form the confession takes in the Johannine tradition of John 6:67–69). In favor of an affirmative deduction of some sort is the obvious rebuke of Peter by Jesus (modified in Matthew 16:17–19 and mollified in Luke 9:22). Yet if Peter did historically admit that Jesus was the "messiah" at Caesarea Philippi, one has to grant that the implication of that title was not yet what it became for post-resurrection Christianity. Jesus' rebuke of Peter at least meant the rejection of the political overtones associated with the title. (See §14 above.)

Again, in Mark 14:62, in the course of the interrogation before the Sanhedrin, Jesus is depicted giving an affirmative answer to the high priest's question, "Are you the messiah?" But that frank affirmative Marcan answer has a parallel in Matthew 26:64 ("You have said so," i.e. that is the way you put it; cf. Lk 22:67–70), with either only a half-affirmative answer or a non-committal response. Not only do the parallels raise a question about the form of that historic answer, but this part of the passion narrative is not without its Marcan editorial concerns and redaction. It gives little basis for a judgment about Jesus' own messianic consciousness.

By the time that Paul wrote, "Christ" had already become a proper name, save in Romans 9:5. This Pauline use shows that this title was the most primitive and the most frequently used. It was most likely Pilate's inscription on the cross, "The King of the Jews" (Mk 15:26), that served as the catalyst for the use of "messiah" for a crucified anointed agent of Yahweh. The pre-Lucan (and most likely pre-Pauline) tradition embedded in Acts 2:36 suggests that Jesus was so hailed shortly after the resurrection: "This Jesus whom you crucified . . . God has made Lord and Messiah."

Still another early Christian understanding of his messiahship, however, is found in Acts 3:20–22, where God is said to be expected to send "the messiah designated for you, Jesus, whom heaven must welcome until the time for establishing all that God has spoken about by the mouth of his holy prophets of old." This has been called the oldest christology preserved in the New Testament, relating Jesus' messiahship not to his resurrection, but to his parousia. Here he would be still expected to come as "messiah." This understanding of Acts 3:20 is not impossible. It would give a clearer understanding to the process of retrojection of titles from a later phase of Christ's existence to an earlier, which seems at times to have been at work. It may, however, be a remnant of a para-kerygmatic christology, a belief in the parousiac Jesus as messiah, which had some vogue in a part of the early Christian church, but which never caught on or became as influential as the kerygmatic proclamation of him as messiah as of the resurrection. These are reflections of different ways in which early Christians understood Jesus' messiahship and which point mainly to a post-resurrection emergence of the title.

b. The titles "Son of God" and "Lord" are not only of Palestinian Jewish origin, but are also clear examples of confessional titles used of Jesus, which emerged in the post-resurrectional period. Even though *divi filius,* "Son of God," and *kyrios,* "Lord," were titles current in the Greco-Roman world of the time, used of the Roman emperor and/or pagan deities, and may be reflected in such New Testament passages as I Corinthians 8:5 or Acts 25:26, this evidence cannot be claimed as the sole origin of the titles "Son of God" or "Lord" for Jesus in the New Testament writings.

c. There is now evidence to show that "Son of God" was used in Palestinian Judaism in pre-Christian times by Aramaic speakers and that the absolute (i.e. unmodified) use of "(the) Lord" was also attributed to Yahweh himself (see my article, "The Contribution of Qumran Aramaic to the Study of the New Testament," *NTS* 20 [1973–74] 382–407, esp. pp. 386–94; reprinted in *A Wandering Aramean: Collected Aramaic Essays* [SBLMS 25; Missoula, MT: Scholars, 1979] 85–113, esp. pp. 87–94; cf. M. Hengel, *The Son of God* [Philadelphia: Fortress, 1976]).

These, then, are titles that must have quickly emerged as the

kerygma was formulated; they are not solely the product of missionary endeavor, as that kerygma was carried from Palestine to the
eastern Mediterranean Greco-Roman world, as has often been
maintained. When these post-resurrectional titles appear earlier in
the gospel tradition (e.g. Mt 16:16b; Lk 1:32, 35; 2:11; 12:42), they
are to be regarded as retrojections of the evangelists who used of the
earthly Jesus titles current for him in the post-resurrection period or
in their own day (see the discussion on "Son of the living God" in
§14g above).

   d. The greatest debate at present surrounds the title "Son of
Man." In the vast majority of instances it is found on the lips of
Jesus himself; but it is used of him by others in Acts 7:56 (by Stephen), John 12:34 (by the crowd), and Mark 2:10 and par. (by the
evangelist[s], even though in this last case many commentators use
subterfuges, such as anacoluthon [expressed by dashes], to claim
that this instance too appears on his lips). Because "Son of Man"
does so appear in many cases, the question arises whether Jesus
actually used the Aramaic term *bar 'enāš* or *bar 'enāšā'* in his ministry to refer indirectly to himself. This is a legitimate question, even
if one has to realize that the title has been secondarily introduced
into certain passages by an evangelist, where the parallel passage
lacks it (cf. Mk 8:27c ["Who do people say that I am?"] and Mt
16:13 ["Who do people say that the Son of Man is?"]; similarly Lk
6:22 and Mt 5:11).

   "Son of Man" is found in both the Johannine and the synoptic
traditions (with different nuances, to be sure), and it does not purport to be a confessional title. It plays no role in the christology of
other New Testament writings, save in the book of Revelation. The
awkward Greek phrase *hō huios tou anthrōpou* (literally, "the son of
the man") scarcely permits one to derive this title from a Hellenistic
background. Because it sometimes occurs without the definite articles (*huios anthrōpou* [e.g. Jn 5:27]) and resembles a Semitic

construct-chain, it is usually regarded as a translation of *bar 'enāš,*
which does occur in contemporary Aramaic texts in a generic sense
(= human being) or an indefinite sense (=someone). But its denotation in contemporary usage is highly disputed.

Was it a title for an expected apocalyptic figure in pre-Christian
Palestinian Judaism? A mere development from a non-titular synonym (= "human being" or "someone") or from a substitute-expression for "I" or "he"? There is no evidence in Aramaic for the
use of "Son of Man" as a title for an individual expected or apocalyptic figure. In Daniel 7:13 the phrase occurs, but it is a designation
for the corporate "saints" of Israel. The titular use of the phrase in
Enochic literature (*1 Enoch* 46:2–4; 48:2; 62:9, 14; 63:11; 69:26–27,
29; 70:1; 71:14) is likewise contested. The substitution of "Son of
Man" for "I" in some New Testament passages (see above) has
raised the question about the phrase as a substitute expression. This
use is found in some Aramaic writings of later centuries (scarcely
before A.D. 300), but as yet has not been found in any contemporary Aramaic texts. In my opinion, the titular use of the phrase for
Jesus in the New Testament is best explained as a development in
the early Christian community from sayings in which he used the
phrase "Son of Man" of himself in a non-titular and non-substitute
sense, meaning nothing more than "a human being." In the pre-written Greek gospel tradition it then assumed a titular sense, and
that is why it was preserved in its barbarous Greek form. The connotations that the phrase carries in various New Testament contexts,
however, have to be scrutinized individually.

Finally, the title is applied to Jesus in the synoptics in three
main ways: (1) it is used of Jesus in his lowly, earthly condition (Mt
8:20; Lk 9:58); (2) it is used of him in reference to his passion (lacking in "Q," but see Mk 8:31; 9:31; 10:33); and (3) it is used of him
coming in glory or judgment ("Q": Mt 24:27; Lk 17:24; Mk 8:38;
13:26). Though each of these three senses is transmitted in the gos-

pel tradition, it is not possible to establish any real connection among them. In my opinion, it is highly unlikely that Jesus himself ever used the phrase as a title of some expected figure apart from himself (for the reason stated above).

23. After the Resurrection Was Jesus Proclaimed Unambiguously from the Start as Son of God, Equal to the Father?

a. The earliest use of "Son" for Jesus in the New Testament is found in what is usually regarded as a pre-Pauline kerygmatic fragment in Paul's first letter, 1 Thessalonians 1:10: "to wait for his Son from heaven, whom he raised from the dead, Jesus who delivers us from the wrath to come." In a similar fragment (Rom 1:3–4) there is a double use of "Son": the first may be Pauline and refer to Jesus as pre-existent, whereas the second, the pre-Pauline usage, speaks of his being constituted or appointed "Son of God in power" as of (his) resurrection from the dead. Elsewhere in Paul's writings we find reference to Jesus as God's "Son" (e.g. Gal 1:16; 4:6; 1 Cor 15:28; Rom 8:32). In later New Testament writings this title continues in use. The Pauline references, however, show that it did not take long for Christians to recognize Jesus' relationship to Yahweh precisely under this title. M. Hengel (in the book cited in §22c above) argues strongly that this belief emerged between A.D. 30 and 50.

b. Was the title used of him "unambiguously from the start"? This is not easy to say. Even those New Testament interpreters who would regard some of the early speeches in Acts as reflecting the primitive kerygma, a view that is not universally admitted, would have to agree that "Son" is hardly a title associated with this form of the kerygma. The early chapters of Acts use many titles of Jesus (see §17c above), some of which are pre-Lucan, but "Son" appears only in Paul's preaching (Acts 9:20 and 13:33 [the latter in a quotation from Psalm 2:7, applied to the risen Christ]).

c. Even if one asserts that "Son" was a title used very early of

Jesus, it is not easy to say that it meant "equal to the Father." Of
itself it implies subordination, that of a natural son to his father.
Jesus, however, was not *'abbā'*, and in its confession of Jesus the
New Testament never identifies him with the Father (see §17
above). (He is one with the Father in the Johannine claim of 10:30.)
But 1 Corinthians 15:25–28 speaks openly of his subjection even as
"the Son himself" (cf. Heb 1:2–8). Yet in giving him the title *kyrios*,
a title used of Yahweh in Palestinian Judaism (see Ps 114:7;
11QtgJob 24:7; 1QapGen 20:12–13, 4QEnoch^b 1 iv 5; Josephus,
Ant. 20.4,2 §90; 13.3,1 §68), it implied that he was somehow on a
level with Yahweh, without, however, being identified with him or
made absolutely equal to him (*Gleichsetzung,* not *Identifizierung!*).

d. The phrase "equality with God" is used of Jesus in the pre-
Pauline hymn in Philippians 2:6. But it is quite disputed in what
sense that phrase is to be understood: whether that equality was
something that was his and that he did not hesitate to give up (in his
kenōsis), or was something that he did not have and did not even
grasp after. Yet even so, it is precisely these ambiguous New Testament phrases that led in time to the clearer reconceptualization and
reformulation of the relationship of him to God that we know about
from later christological and trinitarian teaching of the patristic period. If it were not for this ambiguity of the New Testament usage,
how would Christians ever have come to the idea of three distinct
persons in the Trinity? Yet that same hymn clearly states that God
gave him a name which was above every other name (viz. *Kyrios,*
"Lord") and that he was accorded the adoration of every knee in
creation (using a phrase that speaks of the same kind of adoration of
Yahweh, in Is 45:23).

e. The notion of Jesus as "Son" is also found in the Johannine
tradition. It is almost certainly not to be regarded solely as the addition of the final redactor(s) of the fourth gospel. There is, however, a
peculiarly Johannine cast to the use of "Son" in this gospel which
prevents one from predicating this usage of Christian belief "from
the start." Even though the assertion of Jesus' oneness with the

Father is expressed in various ways (10:30, 38; 17:5, 21), it has to be understood primarily of a functional christology (i.e. of a belief in the meaning of Christ and the Father for human beings). Yet the Christian reflection and meditation present in this gospel are likewise a prime factor in the gradual development of explicit ontological christology (i.e. a belief in the intrinsic constitution of Christ and of his relation to the Father).

24. In What Sense Can It Be Said That Jesus Was the Redeemer of the World?

From the standpoint of the New Testament the question could be understood in two ways.

a. It could refer to the cosmic dimension of redemption. In the New Testament *kosmos* can denote the world as the "ordered universe" (Jn 17:5; Lk 11:50; Acts 17:24; 1 Cor 8:4). Paul sees the effects of the Christ-event spilling over and influencing not only human beings, but even material or physical creation in general. In Romans 11:15 he speaks of the "reconciliation of the world" (a slogan not further explained in this passage, in which he is treating of Israel's place in or relation to the divine plan of salvation). He may be echoing there 2 Corinthians 5:19, where he says that "God was in Christ reconciling the world to himself." In both of these passages Paul seems to view the Christ-event as having an effect not only on human beings but on the created universe itself. Compare what he says about the "eager longing" of material "creation" (*ktisis*) and its relation to the inward groaning of Christians awaiting the "redemption of their bodies" (Rom 8:19–23). Though it is not easy to explain further this cosmic dimension of redemption, Paul's words have a peculiar ring today, when we hear so much about ecology and reflect on what human beings in their greed, lack of concern for others, and profligacy have been doing to God's good earth. Environmental control is something that has been born of modern industrial and technological society, but perhaps Paul sensed an analogous need of something similar in the world in which he lived, devoid of the effects of so-called modern progress.

b. The question could refer to the universe of human beings or to the application of the effects of the Christ-event to all humanity. Paul, for instance, indicts all human beings: "Since all have sinned and fall short of the glory of God, they are justified by his grace as a gift, through the redemption which is in Christ Jesus" (Rom 3:23–24). In that context Paul was thinking of Jews and Greeks without the gospel: "All human beings, both Jews and Greeks, are under the power of sin" (3:9; cf. 11:32). Taking a cue from other New Testament passages, such as 1 Timothy 2:4–5 (God "desires all human beings to be saved and to come to the knowledge of the truth; for there is one God and one mediator between God and humans, the man Christ Jesus, who gave himself as a ransom for all"), Christian theologians have easily and rightly concluded to the role of Jesus as the redeemer of the world, i.e. of the universe of human beings. This is at least the thrust of much New Testament data that bear on this topic; recall the "universalism" of salvation in Lucan writings or the Johannine stress on the salvation of the world (4:42; 12:47).

c. What bearing does the New Testament material have on the salvation of peoples of other cultures not specifically influenced by Christianity? That question is more properly addressed to a systematic theologian, because it is not within the purview of the New Testament writings. Even the "other sheep who are not of this fold" (Jn 10:16) cannot be extended to all non-Christians without further ado, since there is some likelihood that within the Johannine writings that verse refers to other Christians who were not accepting the Johannine view of the Christ-event with its "high" christology and "closed" ecclesiology. (See further R.E. Brown, *The Community of the Beloved Disciple* [see §12d above].)

d. A specifically acute problem in this regard that Christian theologians have to work out better is the salvation of the Jews. For Christian thinkers have not really developed a satisfactory "theology of Israel." The problem is to explain how a group of people, feeding and nourishing its religious life on two-thirds of what Christians call the Bible, yet not accepting the last third of it and him whom it proclaims, can continue to find its salvation by following the law of Moses, the prophets, and the writings, without accepting him whom Christians call "the redeemer of the world." The problem itself was given a bit of treatment in Romans 9–11, at a very early stage of Christian thinking, but that is scarcely an answer to the existence of Judaism parallel to Christianity in God's plan of salvation for almost nineteen centuries. Moreover, Paul himself admitted that "all Israel will be saved" (Rom 11:26). But he does not say in what way. The meaning of his statement is debated. Some would hold that, since he has not mentioned Christ since Romans 10:17, he means that Israel will be saved by God (Yahweh), and not "through Christ." Then the "deliverer" would be the God of the Old Testament, as in the verse quoted (Is 59:20). (This is the so-called *theo*logical interpretation of 11:26.) Others stoutly maintain that Paul has not conceived of two different modes of salvation, one for Jews, and one for Greeks, but that all are to find salvation "through Christ." (This is the so-called *christo*logical interpretation of that verse.) Whichever is the correct meaning, it bears on the idea of Christ Jesus as the redeemer of the world.

25. Did Jesus Found the Church?

a. In the New Testament "the church" is an entity known in the earliest writings of Paul (e.g. 1 Thess 1:1; 2:14; Gal 1:2, 13, 22; 1 Cor 1:2; 4:17; 6:4; 7:17; 10:32). In the Pauline letters the term *hē ekklēsia* sometimes denotes a local church in a certain area, but in time it comes to denote also "the church" in a transcendent sense, i.e. transcending local or geographical boundaries. Similarly, in later books of the New Testament (Acts 5:11; 8:1, 3; 9:31; 11:22, etc.; Heb 2:12; 12:23; Jas 5:14; 3 Jn 6, 9, 10; Rev 1:4, 11, 20; 2:1, 7, 8, 12,

18, 23; 3:1, 7, 14; 22:16). Significantly, there is no mention of "the church" either in a local sense or a transcendent sense in the gospels of Mark, Luke, or John, or in various other New Testament writings (2 Timothy, 1 and 2 Peter, 1 and 2 John); in Romans the term appears only in chapter 16 (vv. 1, 4, 5, 16, 23) and then only in the sense of a local church. The only gospel in which it is mentioned is Matthew (16:18; 18:17), to which there is no parallel in the other canonical gospels. Such data create a problem and give rise to the question posed.

b. That Jesus had followers is evident from all the gospels (Mk 1:18; 2:15; 6:1; Mt 4:20; Lk 5:11, 28; Jn 1:37, 40). Indeed, he often invited or summoned people to follow him (Mk 1:17; 2:14; Mt 4:19; 9:9; 10:1; Lk 6:12; Jn 1:39). This invitation or summons was the significant beginning of the Jesus-movement. In time his followers came to be called "disciples," i.e. those taught by Jesus (Mk 2:15–16, 23; 3:7–9; Mt 5:1; 10:1; Lk 6:13; 9:1; Jn 2:2), and even "apostles," i.e. those sent forth by Jesus to carry on his mission (Mk 6:30 [sole mention]; Mt 10:2 [sole mention]; Lk 6:13 ["called his disciples and chose twelve of them whom he also named apostles"]; 9:10; 22:14. (*Apostolos* occurs only in a generic sense in the Johannine gospel [13:16], used of Jesus himself.) Thus this invitation to followers or disciples and the commission of them to preach in his name are depicted as the kernel of Jesus' ministry in the New Testament. It is the basis of the apostolate that Paul will eventually consciously carry out. After Jesus' death and burial such followers continued to express their allegiance to him (Acts 1:2, 13–14, 15 [where they are called "the brethren"]; cf. Jn 20:19; 21:14). And the risen Christ poured out his Spirit upon them to continue his work, and soon they went forth and preached in his name (Acts 2:14–36).

c. It is evident from the New Testament that such followers/disciples/apostles were not aware of themselves at first as "the church." Indeed, the most primitive references to them in Acts describe them simply as "the brethren" (1:15) or collectively as "the fellowship" (*hē koinōnia,* 2:42), "the way" (*hē hodos,* 9:2; 19:9, 23;

22:4; 24:14, 22). In the Lucan story the name "church" emerges (Acts 8:1, 3), but at first it designates local groupings of the brethren or disciples (at Jerusalem, 5:11; 11:22; even elsewhere, 11:26; 14:23). In time an awareness of *ekklēsia* as transcending local boundaries also emerges (15:22). Again, in the early letters of Paul "the church(es) of God" (1 Thess 2:14; Gal 1:13) is not necessarily to be understood as a designation of the universal church, since it often refers to the mother-communities of Jerusalem or Judea (1 Thess 2:14; 1 Cor 11:16). This designation is eventually extended to the Corinthian community (1 Cor 1:2; 2 Cor 1:1), and in the Pauline letters the idea of *ekklēsia* as universal church also emerges (1 Cor 6:4; 10:32). It is further found clearly in the deutero-Pauline Col 1:18, 24; Eph 1:22; 3:10, 21, even though it is never said to be *mia ekklēsia,* "one church," even in Ephesians, the letter that teaches above all the uni(ci)ty of the Christian church.

d. Only in Matthew 16:18 is there mention of Jesus "founding" a "church": "You are Peter (*Petros*) and on this rock (*petra*) I will build my church." The scene of Peter's confession (Mt 16:13–19) has its parallel in the earlier gospel of Mark (8:27–30) and in Luke (9:18–20), but in neither of these gospels is there any mention of Jesus founding a church. Moreover, even in the remote parallel to the scene of Peter's confession in the Johannine gospel (6:67–69) there is no mention of such a founding. Thus the gospel evidence about this activity of Jesus is ambivalent.

e. Today it is realized that Matthew 16:16b–19 is a retrojected version of an episode that in the gospel tradition was more likely rooted in a post-resurrection appearance of the risen Christ (see §14 above). Cf. John 21:15–17, which provides a post-resurrection setting for a conversation of Jesus and Simon Peter, which is also church-founding, even though "the church" is not mentioned; yet the role of Peter in the "flock" of Christ (see Acts 20:28) is there spelled out in a way analogous to that in Matthew 16:16–19. Hence, Matthew 16:16–19 is undoubtedly a synoptic version of that "feed my lambs/sheep" incident that Matthew has cast in a pre-resurrection setting.

f. Such an analysis of the Matthean Caesarea Philippi episode does not deny that Jesus founded a "church," but it reveals rather that the awareness that the disciples of Jesus had of themselves as "flock" or "church" was something that developed in the course of the decades between A.D. 33 and A.D. 80–90, when the Matthean and Johannine gospels were composed. In other words Matthew has interpreted with hindsight the real meaning of Peter's confession of Jesus as the messiah (*Christos*) and the implications of Jesus' reaction to it. Matthew has thus depicted the earthly Jesus conferring on Peter a special role in that "church" (= "flock"). Thus the disciples that Jesus invited to follow him and the apostles whom he sent out to share in his mission logically became in time "the church" that he "founded." In this way the "church" is the organic outgrowth or continuity of the Jesus-movement, even though Jesus himself in his earthly ministry may never have had detailed knowledge of how that movement that he started would develop or even a blueprint of its structure.

APPENDIX

1.

The Biblical Commission and Its Instruction on the Historical Truth of the Gospels

The Biblical Commission

In 1902, by his Apostolic Letter *Vigilantiae*[1] Pope Leo XIII established the Pontifical Biblical Commission.

At that time Leo XIII gave the Commission the twofold task of *promoting* biblical interpretation in agreement with his encyclical *Providentissimus Deus*[2] and of *guarding* the Bible against false interpretations. His apostolic letter began with the word "Vigilantiae" (watchfulness, vigilance), and the watchdog aspect of the Commission prevailed, reflecting the troubled period in which it was set up. Though the Biblical Commission was not a Roman congregation in the strict sense, it was organized like one of the curial congregations (with cardinal members and expert biblical consultors).

Under Pope Pius X its task was determined anew. The Commission was to exercise its watchfulness by answering questions from Catholics about biblical problems. This it did above all by *responsa,* the technical term for its more-popularly-called decrees. These responses were usually stylized in the form of questions, often loaded, to which a brief answer was given, either *negative* or *affirmative.* The series of fourteen *responsa* issued between 1905 and 1915 became the hallmark of the Commission. They treated such matters as the following: the theory of implicit quotations; the theory of apparently historical narratives; the Mosaic authorship of the Penta-

---

1. *ASS* 35 (1902–3) 234–38; *EnchBib* §137–38; cf. A. Kleinhans, *LTK* 2. 359–60.
2. *ASS* 26 (1893–94) 269–92; *EnchBib* §81–134; DS §3280–94.

teuch; the author and historical reliability of the fourth gospel; the character of the book of Isaiah; the historicity of Genesis 1–3; the author and date of the Psalms; the authorship, date, and historicity of the gospels of Matthew, Mark, and Luke; the synoptic problem; the authorship, date, and historicity of Acts; the authorship and integrity of the pastoral letters; the authorship and composition of the epistle to the Hebrews; the parousia in Pauline writings.[3] As a result of these *responsa* a dark cloud of fear and reactionary conservatism settled over Roman Catholic biblical scholarship during the first half of the twentieth century.

The decrees of the Biblical Commission were not infallibly issued. Pius X explained that they were "useful for the proper progress and the guidance of biblical scholarship along safe paths," but he did require of Catholics the same submission as similar papally approved decrees of other Roman congregations.[4] Thus was formulated their utilitarian and practical aim.

In the midst of World War II Pope Pius XII issued an encyclical

---

3. These and other early utterances can be found in *EnchBib* §160–61, 181–84, 187–89, 276–80, 324–31, 332–39, 383–89, 390–400, 401–6, 407–10, 411–13, 414–16; *RSS,* 117–38. For a modern commentary on these *responsa,* see T.A. Collins and R.E. Brown, "Church Pronouncements," *NJBC,* art. 72, §25–28. For a few later utterances of the Commission, less pertinent to the topic under discussion here, see *EnchBib* §522–33, 535–37, 582–610, 622–33; *RSS,* 138–49, 154–72; cf. *NJBC,* art. 72, 29–33.

4. Motu proprio *Praestantia sacrae Scripturae* (ASS 40 [1907] 723–26; *EnchBib* §268–73; DS §3503; *RSS,* 40–42): ". . . all are obliged in conscience *to submit* to past and future decisions of the Biblical Commission *in the same way as to the decrees which pertain to doctrine issued by* [*other*] *sacred congregations and approved by the pope*" (§271). This clarification was repeated in a *responsum* of the Commission itself issued on 27 February 1934 (*AAS* 26 [1934] 130–31; *EnchBib* §519; cf. B.N. Wambacq, "Pontifical Biblical Commission." *NCE,* 11. 551–54). There ensued a discussion among theologians of the time about the character of the responses of the Commission, whether they were disciplinary or doctrinal. The majority seemed to think that they were not merely disciplinary, but "indirectly doctrinal." There was also a discussion whether they were concerned with *veritas,* "truth," or *securitas,* "security." See L. Pirot, "Commission biblique," *DBSup,* 2. 111–13.

on the promotion of biblical studies, *Divino afflante Spiritu* (1943).[5] Since that time the Biblical Commission began to play a more open-minded role in promoting Catholic biblical scholarship. Its *responsa* gradually gave way to "letters" and "instructions," which, though they sometimes expressed cautions about popular errors or excessive tendencies, gradually assumed a more positive character. The changed image became apparent in January 1948, when the Commission issued a nuanced answer to a (real) question addressed to it by Cardinal Suhard of Paris about the character of the first eleven chapters of Genesis.[6] In 1951, when the Commission revised the list of topics for examinations to be taken to obtain ecclesiastical biblical degrees, it significantly dropped its own (formerly required) decrees.[7]

To many, both inside and outside the Catholic Church, however, the decrees seemed to be still in effect and the Commission seemed to be still the vigilance committee of old. In 1955 a semi-official explanation of the character of the decrees was issued. The secretary of the Commission, A. Miller, O.S.B., reviewed in *Benediktinische Monatsschrift* a newly revised edition of *Enchiridion biblicum,* a collection of church documents concerning biblical interpretation that had been published across the centuries.[8] At the same time, the subsecretary of the Commission, A. Kleinhans, O.F.M., did the same in the Roman periodical *Antonianum.*[9] Both reviewers, though they wrote in different languages (the former in German, the latter in Latin), significantly used in paragraphs of identical wording an important distinction about the *responsa.*

---

5. *AAS* 35 (1943) 297–326; *EnchBib* §538–69; DS §3825–31; cf. *NJBC,* art. 72, §20–23.

6. *AAS* 40 (1948) 45–48; *EnchBib* §577–81; *RSS,* 150–53; cf. *NJBC,* art. 72, §31.

7. *AAS* 43 (1951) 748; *EnchBib* §638. Compare *AAS* 3 (1911) 48.

8. "Das neue biblische Handbuch," *BenMon* 31 (1955) 49–50.

9. "De nova Enchiridii biblici editione," *Anton* 30 (1955) 53–65.

They distinguished those that touched on faith and morals from those that dealt with literary criticism, authorship, integrity, date of composition, historicity, and similar questions. The former were said to be still valid; the latter were to be regarded as time-conditioned and corresponding to an historical context no longer existent. The two secretaries of the Commission frankly stated that Catholic scholars could in matters related to the latter group of decrees pursue their investigations, research, and interpretation "with full freedom" (*in aller Freiheit, plena libertate*). The significance of this distinction was not lost on Roman Catholic interpreters and was even brought to the attention of Protestant scholars.[10]

10. See E.F. Siegman, "The Decrees of the Pontifical Biblical Commission: A Recent Clarification," *CBQ* 18 (1956) 23–29. For a different view of the distinction made by the secretaries of the Commission, see J.E. Steinmueller, *A Companion to Scripture Studies* (3 vols.; rev. ed.; New York: Wagner, 1969) 1. 301; he accuses Siegman of having "falsely concluded that the decrees have been tacitly revoked and are now only of historical interest." He goes even further in a more recent publication (*The Sword of the Spirit* [Waco, TX: Stella Maris Books, 1977] 7 n. 1) in maintaining that the articles of Miller and Kleinhans were unauthorized and the two secretaries were to be brought before the Holy Office because of these articles but were saved from this ordeal through the personal intervention of Cardinal Tisserant before the Holy Father. This is the recollection of an old conservative, first published twenty-two years after the fact. Why did this allegation not emerge sooner? The point is that, as Steinmueller reveals, the secretaries were not brought before the Holy Office; such a political move was thwarted. Steinmueller's can scarcely be regarded as "the real explanation," *pace* J.P. O'Reilly (*The Priest* 36 [1980] 6). Here the principle *tacere est consentire* is valid; failure to speak against the secretaries equals consent to their affirmations.

That Siegman's interpretation of the clarification is correct may be shown in various ways. A very similar interpretation was given in Europe by J. Dupont, O.S.B., "A propos du nouvel Enchiridion biblicum," *RB* 62 (1955) 414–19. Moreover, many Roman Catholic interpreters of no little stature have been acting in their study and research on such an interpretation, and not a few of them have subsequently been named either consultors or members of the Biblical Commission itself. Such a respected French Dominican Old Testament scholar as A.M. Dubarle had even managed to publish a letter about the matter, prior to this semi-official clarification, in the leading German Protestant biblical periodical in order to offset the views of outsiders about the freedom of Catholic exegetes; see "Lettre à la rédaction," *ZAW* 66 (1954) 149–51.

As a matter of fact, almost all the decrees of the Biblical Commission issued between 1905 and 1915, at the height of the reaction to modernism, belong to the second category. Say what one will about the character of the distinction made by the two secretaries of the Commission, the advances made by Catholic biblical scholars in the last thirty-five years and the acceptance of their work in non-Roman Catholic circles reveal the validity and significance of that distinction.

Since the encyclical *Divino afflante Spiritu* and the letter sent to Cardinal Suhard, the Biblical Commission has issued an instruction about the treatment of biblical subjects in seminaries and houses of theological study of religious orders and congregations (1950)[11] and a Declaration (1953) about a book on the Psalms.[12]

In June 1961 a Roman *monitum* was issued concerning the historicity of the Bible.[13] Significantly enough, it came not from the

---

The reader should beware of the summary of the clarification given in *RSS,* 175–76, which omits all reference to the crucial phrases, *in aller Freiheit, plena libertate,* "with all freedom."

11. *AAS* 42 (1950) 495–505; *EnchBib* §582–610; *RSS,* 157.

12. *AAS* 45 (1953) 432; *EnchBib* §621.

13. *AAS* 53 (1961) 507; *RSS,* 174 (the reader should again beware of the tendentious title put on the translation here; the *monitum* was not addressed solely to "biblical scholars").

The text of the *monitum* reads:

"Though biblical studies are progressing in a praiseworthy manner, assertions and opinions are circulating here and there that call in question the proper historical and objective truth [*germanam veritatem historicam et obiectivam*] of sacred scripture, not only of the Old Testament (as Pope Pius XII had already sadly noted in his encyclical 'Humani Generis' [cf. *AAS* 42 (1950) 576]), but also of the New, even with regard to the words and deeds of Christ Jesus.

"Since such assertions and opinions create anxieties for both pastors and the faithful, the cardinals who are charged with the protection of doctrine on faith and morals have considered it necessary to warn all those who deal with the sacred writings either orally or in writing to treat so great a subject with prudence and reverence. Let them always pay attention to the teaching of the fathers, the mind of the church, and the magisterium, lest consciences be disturbed or truths of the faith be harmed.

Appendix

Biblical Commission, but from the Holy Office (as the Congregation for the Doctrine of the Faith was then called). An appended brief note recorded that the agreement of the cardinals of the Biblical Commission had been obtained for the *monitum.* Nevertheless, it was clear that the watchdog role was now being played by a different Roman congregation.

By this time the Biblical Commission itself had gone through a process of opening up, leading to the positive promotion of biblical studies. In 1963 five distinguished European biblical scholars, noted for their openness to modern interpretation of the Bible, were associated with the Commission as consultors: R. Schnackenburg (Germany), C. Spicq, O.P. (Switzerland), X. Léon-Dufour, S.J. (France), B. Rigaux, O.F.M. (Belgium), and G. Castellino, S.D.B. (Italy). This list of consultors was further expanded in 1965 by other well-known and respected names of contemporary scholarship: B.M. Ahern, C.P. (United States), R.A.F. MacKenzie, S.J. (Canada), P.W. Skehan (United States), H. Schürmann (East Germany), R. Lach (France), and G. Rinaldi (Italy). In 1964 three new cardinals were added to the Commission, two of whom were biblical specialists: B. Alfrink (Holland), F. König (Austria), and I. Antoniutti (Italy). True, the conservative cardinals A. Ottaviani, E. Ruffini, and M. Browne, O.P. were still retained as members of the Commission, but their influence was now counter-balanced. The image of the Commission itself was gradually changing.

A further step in the change of the image of the Commission was taken in its Instruction of 1964 on the historical truth of the gospels. This Instruction showed that the Commission could concretely handle in a positive way a problem that vexed many modern

---

"This warning is issued with the agreement of the cardinals of the Pontifical Biblical Commission."

Cf. *TS* 22 (1961) 442 for an explanation of *germanam veritatem historicam et obiectivam.*

Christian students of the Bible both in and outside of the Roman communion. In that Instruction a distinction was proposed that is fundamental for the proper interpretation of the canonical gospels by anyone who would try to understand what they are all about.

Before turning to that Instruction, however, we should add two further developments of later date to complete this brief sketch of the role of the Biblical Commission in the modern Roman Catholic Church and of the transformed image projected by it in the last decade and a half. *First,* the fundamental distinction proposed by the Commission in its Instruction of 1964 was adopted by the fathers of Vatican Council II in chapter 5 of the Dogmatic Constitution *Dei Verbum,* which treated of the New Testament and its relation to revelation.[14] Thus the authority of an ecumenical council was added to the proposal made in the 1964 Instruction of the Biblical Commission. *Second,* in 1971 Pope Paul VI completely revamped the Biblical Commission, making it a counterpart of the Theological Commission, associating both of them more closely to the Congregation of the Doctrine of the Faith, and staffing it no longer with cardinals but with twenty members of international background, many of them biblical scholars of recognized competence.[15]

---

14. *Dei verbum* §19; *AAS* 58 (1966) 817–36, esp. pp. 826–27. See pp. 163–64 below.

15. Motu proprio *Sedula cura* (*AAS* 63 [1971] 665–69).—In its newly-constituted form the Biblical Commission has issued no decree or instruction so far, but only a collection of essays and statements on christology and the church (see p. 166). One report prepared by it on New Testament data about the possible ordination of women was leaked to the press; see "Can Women Be Priests?" *Origins* 6 (1976–77) 92–96. Cf. the Sacred Congregation for the Doctrine of the Faith, "Declaration on the Question of the Admission of Women to the Ministerial Priesthood," ibid. 517–24.

The names of the members of the Commission can be found in *Annuario pontificio* each year.

The Instruction of 1964

The Instruction *Sancta Mater Ecclesia* dealt with "the histori-cal truth of the gospels."[16] It treated a problem that had been the concern of many Catholics in the immediately preceding decades, that surfaced in the discussions of the bishops at the beginning of Vatican Council II, and that continues to be of concern to many theologians and lay people. Unfortunately the sage advice that was incorporated in the Instruction has frequently been ignored in the circles where it is needed most.

That an age-old problem had been posed in a new way was evident from the *monitum* of 1961, published by the Holy Office on the same subject.[17] That document, however, was wholly negative in character and shed no light on the problem itself. The Instruction of the Biblical Commission, coming at a time when it did, during the course of Vatican Council II, proved to be, by contrast, a positive document of no little importance. Given the trend of modern Cath-olic gospel studies in the immediately preceding decade and the diverse reaction to them in the church at large, there is reason to study the Instruction in some detail to appreciate its importance.

---

16. The first publication of "Instructio de historica evangeliorum veritate" appeared in *OssRom* 14 May 1964, p. 3 (with an accompanying Italian translation); the definitive publication is found in *AAS* 56 (1964) 712–18. Cf. DS §3999–99e.

An English translation of the Instruction appeared in Catholic newspapers in the United States; because it was faulty in places and unreliable in crucial paragraphs, I appended to the original form of this discussion an improved translation prepared from the Latin text in *OssRom*. This translation, now slightly revised, follows the present commentary. My translation preserves the paragraphing of the original. Only certain paragraphs in the Latin text are numbered with arabic numerals; they have been retained. To facilitate reference to the text of the Instruction, however, I have added roman numerals to all of its paragraphs in my translation.

After this translation and commentary were prepared, the secretary of the Bibli-cal Commission sent out an English version of the Instruction. It can be found in *CBQ* 26 (1964) 305–12; *Tablet* (London) 218 (30 May 1964) 617–19; *TBT* 13 (1964) 821–28; *AER* 151 (1964) 5–11.

17. See n. 13 above.

That the Instruction was a well-nuanced document became evident from newspaper reports announcing its publication; some of the best of them interpreted it in almost diametrically opposed senses. The *New York Times* ran a headline: "Vatican Cautions Students of the Bible; Rejects as Dangerous and Invalid Any Conclusions Not Arising from Faith; Inquiry Limits Defined; Modern Historical Methods Accepted If Scholars Are Wary of 'Prejudices.' "[18] On the contrary, the *New York Herald Tribune* summed up its report under the headline: "Vatican Gives Green Light to Biblical Scholars."[19]

When studied closely, however, the Instruction was seen to be a document that does not commit Catholic students of the gospels to a fundamentalistic literalness in the matter of their historicity. It contains no condemnation of any specific modern opinion about the historical value of the gospels. Though it catalogues in some detail questionable presuppositions of many form critics, this is done to clear the way to a recognition of the permanent value of the form-critical method itself. Consequently, the Instruction is an historic "first," the first official ecclesiastical statement openly countenancing biblical criticism and frankly admitting the distinction of three stages of the gospel tradition, which has emerged from the form-critical study of the gospels.

The Title of the Instruction

The 1964 document is entitled *Instructio de historica evangeliorum veritate,* "An Instruction about the Historical Truth of the Gospels." A close analysis of its text reveals that the most important

---

18. *New York Times,* 14 May 1964, 37 (article written by R.C. Doty). His inaccurate summary of the Instruction was irresponsibly reproduced in great part in *HPR* 64 (1963–64) 773 ("Attention Biblical Scholars").

19. *New York Herald Tribune,* 14 May 1964, 7 (article written by S. de Gramont).

word in the title is not the adjective *historica,* which might have
been one's initial expectation, but the preposition *de,* "about." Significantly, par. III,[20] which states the problem, omits the word "historical": "because many writings are being spread abroad in which
the truth of the deeds and words which are contained in the gospels
is questioned."[21] In the light of the rest of the Instruction the omission of the adjective seems intentional. In fact, though *historica
veritas* appears in the title of the document, it is used only once in its
text, and then in a sentence in which is decried a certain philosophical or theological presupposition of the form-critical method, to
which no Catholic exegete would subscribe anyway.[22] In none of the
positive directives of the Instruction does the phrase "historical
truth" reappear. The Biblical Commission was evidently far more
interested in sketching in broad lines the character of the truth of the
gospels than in just reasserting that the gospels are "historical."

The Structure of the Instruction

After three introductory paragraphs the Commission addresses
directives to (a) exegetes, (b) professors of scripture in seminaries
and similar institutions, (c) preachers, (d) those who publish for the
faithful, and (e) directors of biblical associations. Under (d) ordinar-

---

20. On the numbering of the paragraphs, see n. 16 above.

21. The Latin text runs: ". . . quod multa scripta vulgantur, quibus veritas
factorum et dictorum quae in evangeliis continentur, in discrimen vocatur." This
sentence echoes the wording of the *monitum* of the holy office. But it is noteworthy
that a simpler phraseology has now been used. The *monitum* had complained of
assertions and opinions that were circulating "that call in question the proper historical and objective truth of sacred scripture, not only of the Old Testament . . . but also
of the New, even with regard to the words and deeds of Christ Jesus" (see the full text
in n. 13 above).

22. Par. V (middle). The Latin text reads, "Alii e falsa notione fidei procedunt
ac si ipsa veritatem historicam non curet, immo cum eadem componi non possit."
The immediately following sentence uses the phrase "historicam vim et indolem
documentorum revelationis," an expression which has a wider connotation.

ies (i.e. above all, diocesan bishops) are reminded to be vigilant of publications on scripture. Except for the first group (a), and the omission may be a mere typographical error, the groups addressed are clearly mentioned in italics. In the directives addressed to the exegetes, italics are again used to indicate the three stages of the gospel tradition discussed there. In this way the structure of the document is evident.[23] The conclusion consists of two paragraphs, in the last of which appears the approval of Pope Paul VI, dated 21 April 1964.

The Introduction (Paragraphs I–III)

The church's concern for the scriptures is recalled as the basis and background for all the work of exegetes. They are urged to rely not only on their resources, but also on God's help and the light of the church.

In par. II joy is expressed at the growing number of competent interpreters of the Bible in the church of today. Explicit recognition is made of the fact that they have been following papal encouragements. This clause was obviously incorporated into the Instruction in order to offset the criticism heard at times in Catholic circles that "exegetes" have been undermining the faith with their new interpretations. There follows a counsel to charity needed in this area so peculiarly prone to emotional discussion. It repeats the counsels found in *Divino afflante Spiritu* and *Vigilantiae.* Tucked away between the quotations is the remark that not even St. Jerome was always successful in handling the scriptural difficulties of his time.[24]

---

23. The italics of the original are preserved in my translation of the Instruction so that the structure of the document should be evident. The principle underlying the use of arabic numbers for certain paragraphs, however, changes after a while; though they too have been preserved, they are not a real guide to the structure. My references will always make use of the added roman numerals. On the opening sentence of the Instruction, see G.F. Woods, *TS* 27 (1966) 725.

24. For an example of the troubles which Jerome had, see my resume of an episode in his life concerning the translation of Hebrew *qîqāyôn* of Jonah 4:6, in *TS*

Paragraph III is like a topic sentence. It sets forth the problem to be discussed and states the Commission's purpose in issuing the Instruction.

Directives for Exegetes (Paragraphs IV–XI)

Eight of the following fifteen paragraphs of the Instruction are addressed to exegetes (pars. IV–XI). When these paragraphs are compared with the rest of the document, it is evident that its essential directives are found in this part. The directives for seminary professors, preachers, popular writers, and directors of biblical associations are hortatory and prudential. Exhortations and cautions are, of course, included in the directives to the exegetes, but it is only in this part of the Instruction that one finds directives of a positive, didactic nature.

Paragraph IV begins with an exhortation addressed to "Catholic exegetes" (*exegeta catholicus*). They are counseled to derive profit from *all* the contributions of former interpreters, especially from those of the fathers and doctors of the church. In this they are to follow the example of the church itself. Moreover, they are also urged to utilize the norms of "rational" and "Catholic hermeneutics." What is meant here by "rational" hermeneutics is the universally admitted principles of criticism that prevail in the study of all forms of literature (in contrast to certain "fads" that emerge from time to time). Such principles include the norms of literary and historical criticism that guide any philologian or interpreter of ancient or modern literature or documents. The addition of "Catholic" defines further norms that must guide the Catholic interpreter (e.g. that the Bible is a collection of inspired writings, that genuine revelation is contained in it, that its fundamental purpose is the upbuilding of the people of God, etc.). What is especially meant by

---

22 (1961) 426–27. He used *hedera,* "ivy," whereas older Latin versions had *cucurbita,* "gourd," and Augustine took him to task for it.

the norms of rational and Catholic hermeneutics is further explained by the recommendation of the aids offered by historical
method. In particular, one is singled out from among them. The
Commission urges the exegete once again to study the literary form
used by the sacred writer. The Instruction recalls the words of Pius
XII and stresses that the use of this mode of interpretation is the
exegete's *duty* and that it may not be neglected.[25] Alas, this directive
of the Instruction has not always been heeded in the time since its
publication.

Particularly important is the following sentence of par. IV stat-
ing that a general rule of hermeneutics is applicable to both the Old
and New Testaments: the composition of their books has been
guided by modes of thinking and writing contemporary with their
authors (and not necessarily with those of modern readers). This
indirect reference to the nature of the gospel testimony briefly out-
lines the bulk of the following directives in pars. VII–X. For the
investigation of the modes of speech and of literary forms—in effect,
what is usually referred to as form criticism—cannot be dispensed
with in the interpretation of any biblical books, not even of the

---

25. An outspoken opponent of the study of the literary forms of the Bible was
E. Cardinal Ruffini. He was a member of the Biblical Commission, at the time when
this Instruction was issued, which publicly reiterated the injunction of Pius XII to the
exegetes of the church in *Divino afflante Spiritu* to pursue such study, especially with
regard to the gospels. Cardinal Ruffini's rejection of this type of interpretation can be
found in his article, "Generi letterari e ipotesi di lavoro nei recenti studi biblici,"
OssRom, 24 August 1961, p. 1. Having appeared on the first page of such a prominent
church-organ and having been sent by the Sacred Congregation of Studies and Univer-
sities to the rectors of all Italian seminaries, it was accorded no little respect. It appeared in an English version in many Catholic newspapers in the United States; cf.
"Literary Genres and Working Hypotheses in Recent Biblical Studies," *AER* 145
(1961) 362–65. In this article, published after the death of Pius XII, Ruffini went so
far in his disagreement as to quote Pius XII indirectly and to use the word "absurdity"
in connection with the study of such forms. The present Instruction was meant to put
an end to the confusion that his article created. Cf. H. Fesquet, "Nouvelles querelles
dans les milieux romains de la critique biblique," *Le Monde,* 1 November 1961, p. 8.

canonical gospels. Thus, in the last sentences of par. IV are set forth the guiding principles of the whole Instruction.

First, the interpreter must use "all the means available" in the interpretation of the gospels; no method or means of interpretation may be excluded a priori, but all are to be used in an intelligent way to attain the goal intended. *Second,* it is not so much a question of ensuring at all costs the historical character of every gospel verse as it is of ascertaining the way in which truth has been there presented. One must be more concerned about a better understanding of the peculiar nature of the testimony borne to Jesus Christ in the gospels.

Paragraph IV has thus dealt with the principles, whereas par. V turns to the concrete use of the form-critical method in the study of the gospels. This method was developed by scholars at the beginning of this century in answer to certain definite problems. Today it is no longer a purely methodological theory, but has acquired adult stature. Its infant stages, however, developed only with the most meager involvement of Catholic interpreters; and today the latter bring certain distinctions into the discussion of it. For this reason par. V distinguishes clearly between the "reasonable elements" (*sana elementa*) in the method itself and the questionable "philosophical and theological principles." Such presuppositions have often been closely linked with the method itself and tended to vitiate its conclusions, but they can be separated and have often been so separated in more recent decades. It is impossible to explain here in detail the method itself or the questionable presuppositions.[26] One should

26. For a brief description of the method and a discussion of the problems involved, see A. Wikenhauser, *New Testament Introduction* (New York: Herder and Herder, 1958) 253–77; and, better still, A. Wikenhauser and J. Schmid, *Einleitung in das Neue Testament* (6th ed.; Freiburg im B.: Herder, 1973) 290–96. Or J.L. Price, *Interpreting the New Testament* (2nd ed.; New York: Holt, Rinehart and Winston, 1971) 160–82; A.H. McNeile, *An Introduction to the Study of the New Testament* (rev. ed. C.S.C. Williams; Oxford: Clarendon, 1953) 458; K. Koch, *The Growth of the Biblical Tradition: The Form-Critical Method* (New York: Scribner, 1969) [for application to Old Testament interpretation]; X. Léon-Dufour, "La lecture critique des

note the six specific presuppositions or "principles" listed in the Instruction; they would normally be rejected by Catholic interpreters in any case, since many of them are the heritage of rationalism: (1) the denial of a supernatural order; (2) the denial of God's intervention in the world in strict revelation; (3) the denial of the possibility and existence of miracles; (4) the incompatibility of faith with historical truth; (5) an almost a priori denial of the historical value and nature of the documents of revelation; (6) a disdain for apostolic testimony and undue emphasis on the creative community in the early church.[27]

Having made this distinction between the "reasonable elements" and the "philosophical and theological principles" of past form-critical study, the Biblical Commission goes on in par. VI to another, more important distinction, which is really the fruit of a

---

évangiles," *Introduction à la Bible: Edition nouvelle* (ed. A. George and P. Grelot; Paris: Desclée) 3/2 (1976) 187–207; A. Robert and A. Feuillet, *Introduction to the New Testament* (New York: Desclée, 1965) 287–310; Bp. J.-J. Weber, " 'Formgeschichte': Wert und Grenzen dieser Methode für das Neue Testament," *TheolGeg* 6 (1963) 63–72; reprinted, *Herderkorrespondenz* 17 (1962–63) 425–29.

27. The sixth item seems to be directed against the original German Protestant form critics, whose ideas of *Gemeindetheologie,* "community theology," are apparently being repudiated. See V.T. O'Keefe, "Towards Understanding the Gospels," *CBQ* 21 (1959) 171–89.

There is, of course, a sense in which it is legitimate to say that the early Christian community "created" a story about Jesus. Take, for instance, the question of divorce. The *Sitz im Leben* in the early church(es) may well have been a debate or the solving of some specific case of conscience ("Do we Christians permit divorce or not?"). Words of Jesus on the subject were recalled, and the story (as in Mk 10:2–12 [minus the Marcan adaptation]) was "created" at that time. Such a story was likely to be repeated for a generation, with varying modifications, until it became a norm for deciding similar cases and was incorporated into the gospel tradition proper. For an attempt to sort out the phases of the tradition about this particular example, see my article, "The Matthean Divorce Texts and Some New Palestinian Evidence," *TS* 37 (1976) 197–226; reprinted, *To Advance the Gospel: New Testament Studies* (New York: Crossroad, 1981) 79–111.

A difficulty is sensed in that the expression "created" often connotes fabrication out of whole cloth. For this reason it is perhaps wiser to speak of the "formation" of the story in the early church rather than of its "creation."

sane use of this method as applied to the gospels. This is the distinction for which this Instruction has rightly been praised.

It concerns the "three stages" of the gospel tradition: (I) the origin of the traditional material in the dealings of Jesus with his disciples during his ministry; (II) the passing on and the forming of the material in early apostolic preaching; (III) the shaping of it into written gospels by evangelists. This view of the gospel tradition is adopted by the Commission from previous use of it by Roman Catholic scholars.[28] It enables one to evaluate "the nature of gospel testimony, the religious life of the early churches, and the sense and value of apostolic tradition" (par. IV).

The Instruction speaks of "three stages of tradition" (*tria tempora traditionis*). What is meant has often been referred to by other terms, a difference which serves to bring out other aspects of the problem and its history. Some writers have spoken of three levels of comprehension according to which the gospel text is to be understood; others speak of the three contexts of the gospel material. In the latter case, the expression is a development of the original idea of the *Sitz im Leben* of the German form-critical pioneers. After the First World War they tried to assign to the various gospel stories and episodes a *Sitz im Leben*, a "vital context" in the early church that would have given rise to the story, unit, or episode. For these pioneers, *Sitz im Leben* meant *Sitz im Leben der Kirche*, the setting in the life of the early church. In time, as the debate developed, people

---

28. It would be impossible, and really idle, to try to cite all the Catholic exegetes who have used this distinction in modern times. As an example of some who antedated the Biblical Commission, see J. Dupont, *Les béatitudes* (2nd ed.; Bruges: Abbaye de Saint-André, 1958); B.M. Ahern, "The Gospels in the Light of Modern Research," *ChicStud* 1 (1962) 5–16; D.M. Stanley, "Balaam's Ass, or a Problem in New Testament Hermeneutics," *CBQ* 20 (1958) 556; J.A. Fitzmyer, "The Spiritual Exercises of St. Ignatius and Recent Gospel Study," *Woodstock Letters* 91 (1962) 246–74; reprinted *Jesuit Spirit in a Time of Change* (ed. R.A. Schroth et al.; Westminster, MD: Newman, 1968) 153–81.

For a more recent use of the distinction, see R.E. Brown et al. (eds.), *Peter in the New Testament* (New York: Paulist; Minneapolis: Augsburg, 1973) 10–11.

began to ask about the *Sitz im Leben Jesu,* the vital context in the ministry of Jesus itself, in which the saying or episode might have had its origin in some form or other. Obviously, to recapture this setting with any certainty is a very delicate and difficult undertaking. Finally, modeled on these two *Sitze im Leben* was a third, which is only analogous. Granted that questions about the vital context in the early church or in Jesus' ministry might be legitimate and instructive, nevertheless the important thing is the *Sitz im Evangelium,* the gospel context of the saying or event recorded: How did the evangelist make use of the traditional material that he had inherited or received? No matter what name one might prefer for the three stages or their respective nuances, the same issue is involved: In order to understand what the inspired, canonical gospels are telling us about the life and teaching of Jesus of Nazareth, who has become for Christians Christ the Lord, one has to make this important threefold distinction. Paragraph VI states this expressly in a topic sentence.

Stage I—Jesus' Life and Teaching

Paragraph VII begins with the italicized words *Christus Dominus,* using titles which are more properly characteristic of the second stage. It would have been better to speak here of *Iesus Nazarenus.* In any case, this paragraph deals with the things that Jesus of Nazareth actually did and said, with the things that the chosen disciples saw and heard. Here two things are emphasized: (1) What the disciples saw and heard enabled them to give testimony about Jesus' life and teaching. (2) The technique which Jesus used in teaching was accommodation, intended to make his words understood and retainable. The first few statements in the paragraph are documented with references to the New Testament. The rest of it is a speculative reconstruction, slightly idyllic, but undoubtedly expressing what is essentially to be recalled about this first stage of the gospel tradition.

It is the stage of the *ipsissima verba Iesu,* "the very words of

Jesus." For Christians it has always somehow seemed to be the stage of the greatest importance. What Jesus himself really said would seem to be more important than what the early church passed on as his teaching or what the evangelists report as his sayings.[29] And yet it is noteworthy that the Biblical Commission has not insisted in any way that what we have in the gospels is an exact record of this first stage of the tradition.[30]

Stage II—The Apostles' Preaching

The second stage of the tradition is treated in par. VIII. Once again the emphasis is put on the testimony of the apostles and the accommodations that they made in their message to the needs of those to whom they preached. Even when the Commission says that the apostles after the resurrection "faithfully explained his life and words," it appeals significantly enough to none of the gospels as examples of this faithful explanation, but to a part of one of the speeches of Peter in Acts (10:36–41). Peter's speech (before the conversion of Cornelius and his household) gives a summary of the ministry of Jesus. It has been regarded by C.H. Dodd[31] and others as an example of the early church's kerygmatic preaching. (Mark, the earliest of the canonical gospels, has even been thought to be an expansion of some such summary outline.) Strikingly enough, though no "words" of Jesus are quoted in this speech of Peter,[32] it is

---

29. See further my article, "Belief in Jesus Today," *Commonweal* 101 (1974) 137–42.

30. See pp. 27–28 above.

31. *The Apostolic Preaching and Its Developments* (London: Hodder and Stoughton, 1936; reprinted New York: Harper, 1962). For another view of this matter, see U. Wilckens, *Die Missionsreden der Apostelgeschichte* (WMANT 5; Neukirchen-Vluyn: Neukirchener-V., 1961) 63–70; but cf. J. Dupont, "Les discours missionnaires des Actes des Apôtres: D'après un ouvrage récent," *RB* 69 (1962) 37–60, esp. pp. 39–50.

32. Note, by way of contrast, Acts 20:35, where a saying of Jesus is recorded which did not find its way into the canonical gospels.

still regarded by the Biblical Commission as a "faithful" explanation of Jesus' "life and words." This nuance is not to be overlooked.

In this section the Commission rightly counteracts the idea that the new faith of the apostles after the resurrection and the experience of Pentecost wiped out all authentic recollection of what Jesus did and said, or deformed their impression of him, or volatilized him into some kind of a "mythical" person. The Commission seeks to stress that the New Testament writings, for all their proclamation of Jesus as Lord, assert the *fundamental continuity* between Jesus of Nazareth and Jesus Christ as Lord. Jesus the preacher may well have become the preached one, but this has not developed merely by a Hellenistic process of mythical apotheosis.

Though this questionable conception of the risen Christ is rejected, the Commission insists that the apostles passed on what Jesus had actually said and done "with that fuller understanding which they enjoyed" as a result of the experience they went through at the first Easter and of the illumination of the Spirit of truth at Pentecost. Obvious examples of this *fuller understanding* are quoted from the Johannine gospel (2:22; 12:16 ["His disciples did not understand this at first; but when Jesus had been glorified, then they remembered that what had been written about him was what they had done to him"]; 11:51–52). While these instances are explicitly so identified in the Johannine text itself, the Commission does not imply that this fuller understanding is limited only to these three passages. Rather, it emphasizes that the apostles made accommodations to the needs of the audiences, which led them to rephrase Jesus' sayings and recast their stories about him. Certainly, some differences in the synoptic tradition are owing to this sort of accommodation, which affected the oral tradition in the pre-literary stage, no matter how much leeway one may want to accord the evangelists themselves in the third stage.

Paragraph VIII ends with the mention of "various modes of speaking" that the apostles used in their ministry and preaching. Because they had to speak to "Greeks and barbarians, the wise and the foolish," such contact influenced them and naturally caused further adaptations of the message that they were preaching. By insisting that the "literary forms" employed in such adaptation must be distinguished and properly assessed (*distinguendi et perpendendi sunt*), the Commission has clearly in mind the use of the form-critical method. The forms that are specifically mentioned in the Instruction ("catecheses, stories,[33] testimonia, hymns, doxologies, prayers") are indeed found in the New Testament, but they are not all used in the gospels, at least in any abundance. One thinks more readily of genealogies, parables, miracle-stories, wisdom sayings, appearance stories, infancy narratives, etc. However, the point is made that various literary forms did develop in this stage of the Christian tradition, and that the student of the gospels must learn to distinguish them and assess them. Still more important is the admission by the Commission that there are other forms not specifically mentioned (*aliaeque id genus formae litterariae*), such as were used by the people of that time.

Stage III—The Evangelists' Writing

The longest exposition in the Instruction is devoted to the third stage of the gospel tradition in par. IX. What strikes one here is the emphasis laid on the evangelists' "method suited to the peculiar purpose which each one set for himself." The Commission speaks explicitly of *auctores sacri,* "sacred writers," and leaves the question open whether any of the evangelists might themselves have been

---

33. The Latin word used in the Instruction is *narrationes,* which some may prefer to translate as "narratives." In par. IX it occurs in the singular in the sense of "account," because of its allusion to Luke 1:1. But neither "narrative" nor "account" sufficiently conveys the idea of a literary form, whereas "story" does. It may be objected that this word is "loaded," connoting "fable," "fairy tale," etc. True, it often has this connotation, but not always, nor even necessarily. In the long run, the word "story" does not necessarily connote fiction any more than "narrative" connotes what is factual. I am using "story" without implying any pejorative connotation or value judgment.

"apostles," those of whom it speaks in Stage II. (I speak of "evange-lists" without prejudice to that distinction.) The Biblical Commis-sion reckons with a process of selection, synthesis, and explication at this stage of the gospel tradition. From the stories and sayings, which circulated in stage II, the evangelists selected material to suit their purposes, synthesized it by topical arrangement, and explicated (*ex-planantes*) it to suit the needs of the Christian communities for which they compiled their gospels. Adaptation to the needs of the readers also influenced the process at this stage. Because the evange-lists often transposed episodes to a new context, the interpreter must seek out the meaning intended by the evangelist in narrating a story or recounting a saying of Jesus in the chosen context. In saying this the Commission has implicitly reckoned again not only with form criticism, but also with redaction criticism, a phase of modern gos-pel study that has built upon and added to the earlier form-critical method. Whereas the latter was interested in the history of the liter-ary form (i.e. what the form is and how its development can be discerned as it moves through the tradition), redaction criticism seeks to trace the redactional or editorial history of a saying or epi-sode: How has a given evangelist editorially modified what he has inherited from the tradition before him, and to what purpose (liter-ary, historical, or theological)? This kind of critical study often re-veals much about the theological purpose of the evangelist and tells us about the kind of literary portrait of Jesus that he has been seek-ing to paint, as he utilized and modified inherited material.

After the exhortation to the exegete to ferret out *the evangelist's* meaning, the Commission makes a statement about the "truth" involved in such a process of redaction: "For the truth of the story [*or* narrative, if one insists] is not at all affected by the fact that the evangelists relate the words and deeds of Jesus in a different order and express his sayings not literally but differently, while preserving their sense." The Commission speaks here of "truth" only and does not specify it as "historical truth." One would have to ask what the adjective "historical" would mean in this context after the admission of the redactional modifications practiced by the evangelists. One could, of course, then ask, "Well, if it is not a question of historical truth, of what kind is it?" And the answer would have to be: "gospel truth."[34] (The discussion in par. X will bear this out.) Paragraph IX ends with a quotation from St. Augustine which, even though it comes from a writer who holds a less sophisticated view of the gospels than that being advocated in this Instruction, is nuanced enough to be pertinent to the question. Augustine clearly affirms no naive understanding of the "historical truth" of the gospels. His words as quoted could never support a simplistic equation of stage III of the gospel tradition with stage I thereof.

In par. X, which ends the discussion of the three distinct stages of the gospel tradition, the Commission insists that interpreters will not be fulfilling their task unless they pay careful attention to all the facets of that tradition. It clearly implies, moreover, that the distinction itself is the result of the "laudable achievements of recent re-

---

34. This answer may, of course, sound facetious. It is not meant in the sense in which we commonly use the expression in English: "Now I'll tell you the gospel truth about that." (When this commentary of mine was translated into German as *Stutt-garter Bibelstudien* 1, I warned one of the editors of the series that this answer would be misunderstood in German, unless he sought some way of explaining it. That proved impossible. The booklet was eventually reviewed in *TRev* 63 [1967] 1–8 by an Old Testament professor; he perhaps should be pardoned for what he wrote, but his smugness in criticizing my comments revealed that he had completely missed the point.)

I intend the phrase the "gospel truth" to be taken in a serious way, which the very form of gospel demands. After all truth is analogous; or, as A. Cardinal Bea once put it, "Sua cuique generi literario est veritas" ("Each literary form has its own truth") (*De Scripturae sacrae inspiratione* [2nd ed.: Rome: Biblical Institute, 1935] 106 §90). Truth in a literary text is gauged by the form or genre employed; one has to distinguish historical truth from poetic truth, rhetorical truth from epistolary, hortatory truth from prayer truth (as in the psalter), and legal truth from mythical. In this sense it is legitimate to speak of "gospel truth," i.e. that religious and salutary truth expressed by the evangelist which may indeed make use of historical, or genealogical, or hortatory truth. Since it is difficult to define what a gospel is, it is equally difficult to specify properly in what the gospel truth may consist. In any case, it is not simply identical with "historical truth" in some fundamentalistic sense.

search." Then follows this significant statement: "From the results of the new investigations it is apparent that the doctrine and the life of Jesus were not simply reported for the sole purpose of being remembered, but were 'preached' so as to offer the church a basis of faith and of morals. . . ."[35] The Commission implies thereby that the "gospel truth" is not tied to any fundamentalistic literalness or superior quality of apostolic recollections or reminiscences.

The last paragraph addressed to the exegetes (XI) begins with an admission that there are still many serious problems on which the exegete "can and must freely (*libere*) exercise his skill and genius." The admission about the freedom of exegetical research is a repetition of the statement of Pius XII about the liberty of the Catholic exegete in *Divino afflante Spiritu.* The statement in the Instruction, however, is a paraphrase and contains a significant addition that spells out the relationship of the work of exegetes in the Catholic Church to the magisterium or teaching authority in the church. We juxtapose the two texts:

Divino afflante Spiritu	*Instructio*
There remain therefore many things, and of the greatest importance, in the discussion and exposition of which the skill and genius of Catholic commentators may and ought to be freely exercised, so that each may contribute his part to the advantage of all, to the continued progress of sacred doctrine, and to	There are still many things, and of the greatest importance, in the discussion and exposition of which the Catholic exegete can and must freely exercise his skill and genius, so that each may contribute to the advantage of all, to the continued progress of sacred doctrine, to the preparation and further support of

---

35. The Latin text of this sentence reads: "Cum ex eis quae novae inquisitiones contulerunt appareat doctrinam et vitam Iesu non simpliciter relatas fuisse, eo solo fine ut memoria tenerentur, sed 'praedicatas' fuisse ita ut Ecclesiae fundamentum fidei et morum praeberent, interpres testimonium Evangelistarum indefesse perscrutans, vim theologicam perennem Evangeliorum altius illustrare et quantae sit Ecclesiae interpretatio necessitatis quantique momenti in plena luce collocare valebit" (par. X).

Divino afflante Spiritu	*Instructio*
	the judgment to be exercised by the ecclesiastical magisterium, and to
the defense and honor of the church.[36]	the defense and honor of the church. (Par. XI)

What emerges here in the text of the Instruction is some of the new insights and experiences of Vatican Council II, similar to the awareness expressed by Pope John Paul II in his address at The Catholic University of America in 1979.[37]

Exegetes are finally urged to be ready to submit to the directives of the magisterium, never to forget that the apostles filled with the Holy Spirit preached the good news, and that the evangelists were inspired so that they were preserved "from all error." This final exhortation is supported by a quotation from Irenaeus. So end the directives to the exegetes.

Directives for Professors of Scripture in Seminaries and Similar Institutions

The directives addressed to scripture professors in seminaries and similar institutions (par. XII) consist of an exhortation to teach scripture in a way that the dignity of the subject and the needs of the time require. Coming immediately after the directives to the exegetes, who have been encouraged to pursue a form-critical and redaction-critical interpretation of the gospels, this exhortation implies the seminary professors' duty to cope with the same methods and to engage in the same research. Indeed, this is part of the "needs of the time" (*temporum necessitas*), and such professors cannot ignore them. In reality, the distinction made between exegetes and

---

36. *AAS* 35 (1943) 319; *EnchBib* §565; the translation is from *RSS,* 102.

37. See my discussion in "John Paul II, Academic Freedom and the Magisterium," *America* 141 (1979) 247–49.

seminary professors in this Instruction is largely abstract; the exegete is invariably a professor in a seminary or a similar institution. When, however, the seminary professor is not engaged in this research, such a situation cries out for reform.

The Commission, however, insists that the use of methods of literary criticism is not an end in itself. They must be used to bring out the meaning of the gospel passages intended by God through the sacred writers. The professor is above all to emphasize the theological or religious teaching of the gospels, and literary criticism is to serve only as a means to set forth the theological teaching of the evangelists.[38] Those whom seminary professors are training are future priests and future ministers of the church, for whose lives and work the scriptures must be the source of perennial vitality.

The exhortation in par. XII is predominantly positive. The only negative element in it is a warning against the pursuit of the literary criticism of the gospels as if this could be conceived of as an end in itself.

Directives for Preachers

In the case of preachers the Biblical Commission first insists on their preaching of "doctrine," appealing to 1 Timothy 4:16 (par.

---

38. In the light of these directives it is difficult to understand how some interpreters today can recommend that one abandon the historical-critical method of interpreting the gospels. All through the Instruction it is clear that the modern Catholic exegete and seminary professor are counseled to ascertain and explain what the intention of the inspired writer was and what meaning his message has for people in the world of today. The Instruction has not envisaged more recent fads and trends in interpretation, such as structuralism, or those in hermeneutics, such as the recommendation that what is important is not the intended meaning of the author but what the text, having acquired an autonomy of its own, so it is alleged, may mean to readers today. If there is not a radical homogeneity between what it meant and what it means today, then the latter cannot be called "the Christian message." How a concern for the latter and a disregard of the former can be called serious literary criticism is baffling.

XIII). The first strong, negative directives of the entire Instruction appear here: "They are to refrain entirely from proposing idle and insufficiently established novelties." This prohibition, however, has to be properly understood; for immediately afterward the Commission itself allows for the cautious explanation of "new opinions already solidly established." The problem is obvious. There cannot be a double standard of truth, one for exegetes and seminary scripture professors, and another for the faithful. If I am correct in my understanding of this Instruction, then the recognition which the Biblical Commission has given to literary forms and to the sane use of form-critical and redaction-critical interpretation of the Gospels would put the results of such study under the "opinions already solidly established." They are indeed to be explained to the faithful. But whether one does this in the pulpit, as a preacher at the liturgy of the word, or in an instruction class, is a matter of prudential judgment.

The directives to preachers end with another caution: they are not to embellish biblical events with imaginative details scarcely consonant with the truth.

Directives for Those Who Publish for the Faithful

The same prudence demanded of preachers is now required of all those who would write on biblical subjects at a popular level (par. XIV). They are to concentrate on the riches of God's word and are to consider it a sacred duty never to depart from the common teaching and tradition of the church. They are to exploit, however, the findings of modern biblical research, yet avoid "the rash comments of innovators." A "pernicious itch for novelty" is not to lead them to disseminate unwisely what are only trial solutions to classic difficulties.

The Commission further recalls (par. XV) that books and articles in magazines and newspapers on biblical subjects are to be carefully scrutinized by ordinaries (i.e. diocesan bishops and similar superiors).

Directives for Biblical Associations

Directors of biblical associations or societies are to follow the norms for such gatherings laid down by the Biblical Commission on a previous occasion (par. XVI).[39]

Conclusion of the Instruction

The Biblical Commission notes in conclusion (par. XVII) that if all the directives set forth in its Instruction were to be followed, then the study of sacred scripture in the church would greatly contribute to the benefit of all the faithful. It ends with a quotation from 2 Timothy 3:15–17, the classic New Testament passage setting forth the purpose of "all scripture divinely inspired."

Final Remarks

The significance of this Instruction of the Biblical Commission is best understood, on the one hand, in the light of events which had been taking place in the Roman Catholic Church either shortly before its publication in 1964 or contemporary with it, for it was issued during the course of Vatican Council II and all that that meant for the church. As one looks back at that time from the early 1990s, one can see even greater significance.

Shortly before the publication of the Instruction there emerged a rather bitter strife between some professors at the Lateran University in Rome and those of the Biblical Institute, which centered on aspects of the problem with which the Instruction was eventually to deal, "new investigations" (*novae investigationes,* par. X) of the gospels and other biblical books. That strife need not be rehearsed here,[40] but it was unfortunate because it obscured the important issue of the historical truth of the Bible.

---

39. *EnchBib* §622–33; *RSS,* 168–72.

40. See my article, "A Recent Roman Scriptural Controversy," *TS* 22 (1961) 426–44.

In addition, there were mixed reactions, reported from all over the world, to the new trends in modern Catholic biblical studies. Conservative ecclesiastical circles, in Rome and elsewhere, sought, and still do seek, to commit Catholic interpretation of the gospels to fundamentalism.[41] In this context, the well-nuanced position that the Biblical Commission took in this Instruction is of greatest importance. It not only did not espouse any form of fundamentalism, but gave, in effect, official sanction to many of the new trends in biblical study, and especially in gospel study.[42]

---

41. The first draft of the schema *De fontibus revelationis,* prepared by the theological commission for discussion at Vatican Council II, contained two paragraphs which incorporated the terminology of the *monitum* of the holy office (1961) and leveled anathemas against those who would call in question the proper historical and objective truth of the words and deeds of Jesus *prouti narrantur,* "as they are recounted." These paragraphs were eventually rejected along with the rest of that schema. See J. Ratzinger, "Dogmatic Constitution on Divine Revelation: Origin and Background," *Commentary on the Documents of Vatican II* (5 vols.; ed. H. Vorgrimler; New York: Herder and Herder, 1967–69) 3 (1968) 155–66; cf. A. Grillmeier, "The Divine Inspiration and the Interpretation of Sacred Scripture," ibid. 199–246; B. Rigaux, "The New Testament," ibid. 252–61 (esp. pp. 258–59 on the eventual rejection of a papal suggestion to use *vera seu historica fide digna* instead of *vera et sincera* [which was eventually retained]). In contrast to the original schema, what appears in *Dei verbum* §19 is rather a brief summary of the Biblical Commission's Instruction (see p. 163 below).

42. Though the main directives of the Instruction have been addressed to exegetes, it is evident that dogmatic theologians and others also have to reckon with the directives of this document. We smile today in retrospect at the confidence behind the remarks directed against a professor at the Biblical Institute in Rome in the year 1962, which stated that "there exists a numerous and fairly articulate group convinced that the four Gospels and the Acts of the Apostles are genuine and objectively accurate historical documents, which can be used as such legitimately in the science of apologetics. These individuals insist that they have reason to hold and to teach that the events set forth in these books took place in the very way in which they are described in these works. They hold that the words and the deeds attributed to Our Lord were actually uttered and performed by Him . . ." (J.C. Fenton, "Father Moran's Prediction," *AER* 146 [1962] 192–201, esp. pp. 194–95). Not only is such a view of things contrary to the Instruction of the Biblical Commission, but it displays a naiveté that seems never to have heard of the synoptic problem, not to mention form criticism and redaction criticism.

However, the silence of the Commission about certain matters raises several questions. *First,* practically nothing is said in the Instruction about the synoptic problem, i.e. about how the synoptic gospels are related to or dependent on each other (see p. 9 above). True, in dealing with the redactional work of the evangelists, the Commission admitted that they had used a "method suited to the peculiar purpose which each set for himself," and selected, synthesized, explicated, or transposed accordingly. Obviously, the Commission did not want to take sides in the debate about the solution to the problem, which is so contested today.[43] This knotty problem will probably never be solved to the complete satisfaction of everyone, and the Instruction leaves the debate on this issue open. But the silence of the Commission on this question has made some of its statements sound like an over-simplification, as non-Catholic readers of the Instruction may notice. How can one discuss the problem of the historical value of the gospels without assuming, or at least recognizing, some position in this matter? In speculating about the reasons for the silence of the Commission in this area, I have already suggested that the Commission apparently thought that it could give directives in a way sufficiently generic so as not to close debate on solutions to the synoptic problem.

Second, there is the question of the reinterpretation of the words of Jesus by the evangelists in their redactional work. It has often been suggested in recent times that the evangelists have put on the lips of Jesus a fuller form of sayings than his *ipsissima verba,* or

---

It is evident, however, that recent dogmatic theologians, in their discussions of christology, have actually been seeking to cope with the thrust of the Instruction. See W. Kasper, *Jesus the Christ* (London: Burns & Oates, 1976) 26–40; E. Schillebeeckx, *Jesus* (New York: Seabury, 1979); *Christ* (New York: Crossroad, 1981).

43. See further my article, "The Priority of Mark and the 'Q' Source in Luke," *Jesus and Man's Hope* (Perspective Books 1; 2 vols.; Pittsburgh: Pittsburgh Theological Seminary, 1970) 1. 131–70; reprinted (in revised form), *To Advance the Gospel* (see n. 27 above), 3–40.

that certain verses are to be regarded as the redactional addition(s) of
the evangelists. We may cite the Matthean additions to the beatitudes,[44] and to the "Our Father," or the exceptive phrases in the
divorce texts of the gospel tradition,[45] or even the very knotty problem of Matthew 16:16–19.[46] Significantly the Commission has not
come out against such views in Catholic biblical studies in an otherwise comprehensive statement on the "historical truth of the gospels." Indeed, the Commission is undoubtedly hinting at *this kind*
of redactional activity involved in the reinterpretation of the words
of Jesus, when it says: "From the many things handed down they
selected some things, reduced others to a synthesis, (still) *others they
explicated as they kept in mind the situation of the churches*" (par.
IX, my italics). Such an unfolding, explanation, or explication of
traditional material for the situation of various local churches has to
be reckoned with. For instance, the addition of the exceptive phrases
in the divorce texts of Matthew 5:32 and 19:9 may well reflect a
marriage problem in an early Christian community, predominantly
Jewish Christian, but being infiltrated by converts from the Gentile
world already in marital situations for which the evangelist ex-
presses an exception (cf. Acts 15:20, 29; 21:25).[47] The attitude re-

44. Compare Luke's "Blessed are you poor" with Matthew's "Blessed are the
poor in spirit," Luke's "Blessed are you that hunger now" with Matthew's "Blessed
are those who hunger and thirst for uprightness," etc. See the admirable treatment of
this question by J. Dupont, *Les béatitudes* (see n. 28 above), 209–27; also M.M.
Bourke, "The Historicity of the Gospels," *Thought* 39 (1964) 37–56; J.A. Fitzmyer,
The Gospel According to Luke (AB 28–28A; Garden City, N.Y.: Doubleday, 1981,
1985) 631.

45. See my article cited in n. 27 above, esp. pp. 87–89.

46. See now R.E. Brown et al. (eds.), *Peter in the New Testament* (n. 28 above),
83–101; cf. A. Vögtle, "Messiasbekenntnis und Petrusverheissung: Zur Komposition
Mt 16, 13–23 Par.," *BZ* ns 1 (1957) 252–72; 2 (1958) 85–103; T. de Kruijf, *Der Sohn
des lebendigen Gottes* (AnBib 16; Rome: Biblical Institute, 1962) 82; E.F. Sutcliffe,
"St. Peter's Double Confession in Mt 16:16–19," *HeyJ* 3 (1962) 31–41.

47. See P. Benoit, *L'Evangile selon saint Matthieu* (La sainte Bible [de
Jérusalem]; 3d ed.; Paris: Cerf, 1961) 121; H.J. Richards, "Christ on Divorce," *Scr* 11
(1959) 22–32; cf. n. 45 above.

flected in the Instruction toward this type of problem is most significant.

Third, in a church document on the historical value of the gospels one would have thought that something would have been said about the historical character of the infancy narratives of Matthew and Luke. The debate about this part of the gospel tradition was already a live one within Roman Catholicism before the Instruction was issued and before the debate on inspiration and inerrancy at Vatican Council II. The silence of the Commission on this matter, especially in its treatment of Stage I of the gospel tradition, is eloquent indeed.[48]

Fourth, most noteworthy in the whole document, when all is said and done, is that *the Biblical Commission has calmly and frankly admitted that what is contained in the gospels as we have them today is not the record of the words and deeds of Jesus in the first stage of the tradition, nor even the form in which they were preached in the second stage, but the form compiled and edited by the evangelists.* This form, however, reflects with a certain fidelity the two previous stages, to be sure, and the second more than the first.

For the believing Christian and scholar, it is important to note that the evangelists' redacted and edited form of the sayings and deeds of Jesus is the inspired form. The evangelists were moved by

---

48. The same would have to be said about *Dei Verbum* §19; cf. R.E. Brown, *The Birth of the Messiah: A Commentary on the Infancy Narratives in Matthew and Luke* (Garden City, NY: Doubleday, 1977) 562, esp. n. 11.

For another view of this matter, see J. Redford, "The Quest of the Historical Epiphany: Critical Reflections on Raymond Brown's 'The Birth of the Messiah,' " *Clergy Review* 64 (1979) 5–11. The "critical reflections" amount to nothing more than another gratuitous assertion about the historical character of the annunciation, summed up in a question to boot: ". . . what is more feasible than that he [Luke] had to hand on a tradition, oral or written, of the infancy of Jesus whose original source was Mary, whether she was personally with Luke or not at the time of writing?" (p. 9). Alas, a rhetorical question is no basis for historicity or for what is "feasible."

the Holy Spirit to compile, edit, and write down the accounts as they did. This inspiration guarantees their gospel-truth, which is free from error.

It is good, however, to recall that neither the church in its official pronouncements about the nature of inspiration nor theologians in their speculative elaborations have ever taught that the necessary formal effect of inspiration is historicity. The consequence of inspiration is inerrancy in affirmation, i.e. immunity from error in what is affirmed or taught in the sacred writings for the sake of our salvation (see *Dei Verbum* §11). The opposite of such error is not simply historicity, but truth. Yet truth in a literary text is analogous to the literary form used (see n. 34 above). If a passage in the gospels contains historical truth, it does not simply contain it because it is inspired. The reasons for its historical character will be quite other than the inspired character of the text. Inspiration may indeed guarantee such historical truth as is there, even as it would guarantee the poetic truth of what is affirmed in the hymn to Christ in Philippians 2:6–11. The guarantee is not quantitative, but qualitative and analogous. This has to be stressed even when something is narrated in the past tense under inspiration. The first question which confronts the interpreter in such a case as Mark 14:52 ("and he [the youth] left behind the linen cloth and ran away naked") is whether that statement is meant to record an historical event (real naked flight) or to convey symbolism (the *utter* dereliction of Jesus by his followers); similarly for Mark 15:38 ("the veil in the temple was torn in two, from top to bottom").

Lastly, the inspired truth of the gospels was intended by God in his providence to give us not simply a "remembered" account of the life and teaching of Jesus, but a "preached" form of it, "so as to offer the church a basis of faith and morals" (par. X).

The Instruction of the Biblical Commission has by no means put an end to all the problems regarding the historicity of the gospels. Discussion of them has continued and will certainly carry on, but now with much more freedom. The Instruction has occasioned a number of commentaries on it. We append a list of the more important ones as an aid to further study of it and of the problems to which it is addressed.[49]

49. Anon., "Instruktion der päpstlichen Bibelkommission," *Kirchenblatt für die reformierte Schweiz* 120 (1964) 233–34; A. Bea, "La storicità dei vangeli sinottici," *CivC* 115/2 (1964) 417–36; "Il carattere storico dei vangeli sinottici come opere ispirate," ibid. 526–455 (both reprinted in book form, Rome: Civiltà cattolica, 1964; reprinted again with an Italian translation of the Instruction, *La storicità dei vangeli* [Brescia: Morcelliana, 1964]; cf. *The Study of the Synoptic Gospels: New Approaches and Outlooks* [New York: Harper & Row, 1965]); F.W. Beare, "The Historical Truth of the Gospels: An Official Pronouncement of the Pontifical Biblical Commission," *CJT* 11 (1965) 231–37; W. Beilner, "Zur Instruktion der Bibelkommission über die historische Wahrheit der Evangelien," *BLit* 38 (1965) 3–5; "Die Geschichtlichkeit der Evangelien," *BLit* 40 (1967) 159–76; R. Cardinaels, "Bijbelcomissie en Evangelie," *Revue ecclésiastique de Liège* 50 (1964) 271–81; J. Delorme, "La vérité historique des évangiles," *L'Ami du clergé* 74 (1964) 554–59; M. Didier, "Liminaire [à l'Instruction]," *RDiocNam* 18 (1964) 309–12; A. de la Fuente, "Documento alentador para los estudios de la Biblia," *Ecclesia* 24 (1964) 1103–6; E. Galbiati, "L'Istruzione della Commissione Biblica sul valore storico degli Evangeli," *BeO* 6 (1964) 233–45; "L'Istruzione della Commissione Biblica sul valore storico dei Vangeli," *ScCatt* 92 (1964) 303–310; "L'Istruzione sulla verità storica dei Vangeli e l'insegnamento nei seminari," *Seminarium* 18 (1966) 66–91; S. Gonzáles de Carrea, "El metodo histórico-redaccional en los evangelios sinópticos," *Natura et gratia* 11 (1964) 205–25; W. Harrington, "The Instruction on the Historical Truth of the Gospels," *IER* 103 (1965) 73–87; F. Hoyos, "Historia e historias: A propósito de la instrucción de la Comisión Biblica," *RevistB* 27 (1965) 67–73; J. Kahmann, " 'De historica evangeliorum veritate,' Een nieuwe Instructie van de Bijbelcommissie," *Nederlandsche katholieke Stemmen* 61 (1965) 46–51; C. Kearns, "The Instruction on the Historical Truth of the Gospels: Some First Impressions," *Ang* 41 (1964) 218–34; O. Knoch, "Über die historische Wahrheit der Evangelien . . ." *BKirche* 19 (1964) 146–50; N. Lohfink, "Die Evangelien und die Geschichte: Zur Instruktion der päpstlichen Bibel-Kommission vom 21. April 1964," *SdZ* 174 (1964) 365–74 (reprinted, *Theologisches Jahrbuch 1966* [Leipzig: Benno, 1966] 240–48); (an abridged Swedish form appeared in *Credo* 46 [Uppsala, 1965] 29–33); J. Losada, "La verdad histórica de los Evangelios: La instrucción de la Comisión Biblica," *SalTer* 52 (1964) 612–24, 673–83; R.E. Murphy, "The Biblical Instruction," *Commonweal* 80/14 (1964) 418–20; J.A. O'Flynn, "Instruction of the Biblical Commission," *ITQ* 31 (1964) 240–46; M. Peinador, "Sobre la reciente instrucción de la Comisión Biblica," *Ilustración del clero* 57 (1964) 718–24; J. Radermakers, "Instruction du 21 avril 1964 sur la vérité historique des évangiles: Commentaire," *NRT* 86 (1964) 640–43; R. Rouquette, "De Rome et de la chrétienté: L'Instruction de la Commission biblique,"

The text of the Instruction itself follows.[50] After it will be found a translation of *Dei verbum* §19, which restated in a brief conciliar form the teaching of the Instruction of the Biblical Commission of 1964, and, significantly, not that of the *monitum* of the Holy Office of 1961.

Etudes 321 (1964) 105–10; E. Ruckstuhl, "Die Wahrheit der Evangelien: Erläuterungen zur neuen Instructio der Bibelkommission," *Schweizerische Kirchenzeitung* 132 (1964) 297–99; M. Sabbe, "Een nieuwe Bijbelinstructie," *ColBG* 10 (1964) 413–19; R. Schnackenburg, "Über die historische Wahrheit der Evangelien: Instruktion der päpstlichen Bibelkommission," *TheolGeg* 7 (1964) 197–209; A. Stöger, "Die historische Wahrheit der Evangelien: Kommentar zur Instruktion der päpstlichen Bibelkommission vom 21. April 1964," *TPQ* 113 (1965) 57–79; J. Díaz y Díaz and P. Termes, "Evangelios y comisión biblica," *Enciclopedia de la Biblia* (6 vols.; Barcelona: Garriga, 1963), 3. 299–305.

50. The numbering of the footnotes of the Latin text is generally preserved; occasionally it has been necessary to reverse two of them because of the English word order. Words added in parentheses do not appear in the Latin text; they have been supplied for the sake of the English. See nn. 16 and 23 above. For some strange reason the references to the encyclical *Divino afflante Spiritu* are given in the Latin text of the Instruction to the Italian translation of the encyclical in *AAS;* I have changed them to the corresponding pages of the official Latin text.

2.

Instruction: Text

I. Holy mother the church, "the pillar and bulwark of truth,"[1] has always used sacred scripture in her task of imparting heavenly salvation to human beings. She has always defended it, too, from every sort of false interpretation. Since there will never be an end to (biblical) problems, the Catholic exegete should never lose heart in explaining the divine word and in solving the difficulties proposed to him. Rather, let him strive earnestly to open up still more the real meaning of the scriptures. Let him rely firmly not only on his own resources, but above all on the help of God and the light of the church.

II. It is a source of great joy that there are found today, to meet the needs of our times, faithful children of the church in great numbers who are experts in biblical matters. They are following the exhortations of the supreme pontiffs and are dedicating themselves wholeheartedly and untiringly to this serious and arduous task. "Let all the other children of the church bear in mind that the efforts of these resolute laborers in the vineyard of the Lord are to be judged not only with equity and justice, but also with the greatest charity,"[2] since even illustrious interpreters, such as Jerome himself, tried at times to explain the more difficult questions with no great success.[3] Care should be had "that the keen strife of debate should never exceed the bounds of mutual charity. Nor should the impression be given in an argument that truths of revelation and divine traditions

---

1. 1 Tim 3:15.
2. *DaS* 46 (*AAS* 35 [1943] 319; *EnchBib* §564; *RSS,* 101).
3. See *Spiritus Paraclitus* 2,3 (*AAS* 12 [1920] 392; *EnchBib* §451; *RSS,* 50).

are being called in question. For unless agreement among minds be safeguarded and principles be carefully respected, great progress in this discipline will never be expected from the diverse pursuits of so many persons."[4]

III. Today more than ever the work of exegetes is needed, because many writings are being spread abroad in which the truth of the deeds and words which are contained in the gospels is questioned. For this reason the Pontifical Biblical Commission, in pursuit of the task given to it by the supreme pontiffs, has considered it proper to set forth and insist upon the following points.

IV. 1. Let the Catholic exegete, following the guidance of the church, derive profit from all that earlier interpreters, especially the holy fathers and doctors of the church, have contributed to the understanding of the sacred text. And let him carry on their labors still further. In order to put the abiding truth and authority of the gospels in their full light, he will accurately adhere to the norms of rational and Catholic hermeneutics. He will diligently employ the new exegetical aids, above all those which the historical method, taken in its widest sense, offers to him, a method which carefully investigates sources and defines their nature and value, and makes use of such helps as textual criticism, literary criticism, and the study of languages. The interpreter will heed the advice of Pius XII of happy memory, who enjoined him "prudently . . . to examine what contribution the manner of expression or the literary genre used by the sacred writer makes to a true and genuine interpretation. And let him be convinced that this part of his task cannot be neglected without serious detriment to Catholic exegesis."[5] By this piece of advice Pius XII of happy memory enunciated a general rule of hermeneutics by which the books of the Old Testament as well as the New must be explained. For in composing them the sacred writers

---

4. Apostolic Letter *Vigilantiae* (*EnchBib* §143; *RSS,* 33).

5. *DaS* (*AAS* 35 [1943] 316; *EnchBib* §560; *RSS,* 98).

employed the way of thinking and writing which was in vogue among their contemporaries. Finally, the exegete will use all the means available to probe more deeply into the nature of gospel testimony, into the religious life of the early churches, and into the sense and the value of apostolic tradition.

V. As occasion warrants, the interpreter may examine what reasonable elements are contained in the "form-critical method" that can be used for a fuller understanding of the gospels. But let him be wary, because quite inadmissible philosophical and theological principles have often come to be mixed with this method, which not uncommonly have vitiated the method itself as well as the conclusions in the literary area. For some proponents of this method have been led astray by the prejudiced views of rationalism. They refuse to admit the existence of a supernatural order and the intervention of a personal God in the world through strict revelation, and the possibility and existence of miracles and prophecies. Others begin with a false idea of faith, as if it had nothing to do with historical truth, or rather were incompatible with it. Others deny the historical value and nature of the documents of revelation almost a priori. Finally, others make light of the authority of the apostles as witnesses to Christ, and of their task and influence in the primitive community, extolling rather the creative power of that community. All such views are not only opposed to Catholic doctrine, but are also devoid of scientific basis and alien to the correct principles of historical method.

VI. 2. To judge properly concerning the reliability of what is transmitted in the gospels, the interpreter should pay diligent attention to the three stages of tradition by which the doctrine and the life of Jesus have come down to us.

VII. *Christ our Lord* joined to himself chosen disciples,[6] who

---

6. Mk 3:14; Lk 6:13.

followed him from the beginning,[7] saw his deeds, heard his words, and in this way were equipped to be witnesses of his life and doctrine.[8] When the Lord was orally explaining his doctrine, he followed the modes of reasoning and of exposition which were in vogue at the time. He accommodated himself to the mentality of his listeners and saw to it that what he taught was firmly impressed on the mind and easily remembered by the disciples. These people understood the miracles and other events of the life of Jesus correctly, as deeds performed or designed that human beings might believe in Christ through them, and embrace with faith the doctrine of salvation.

VIII. *The apostles* proclaimed above all the death and resurrection of the Lord, as they bore witness to Jesus.[9] They faithfully explained his life and words,[10] while taking into account in their method of preaching the circumstances in which their listeners found themselves.[11] After Jesus rose from the dead and his divinity was clearly perceived,[12] faith, far from destroying the memory of what had transpired, rather confirmed it, because their faith rested on the things which Jesus did and taught.[13] Nor was he changed into a "mythical" person and his teaching deformed in consequence of the worship which the disciples from that time on paid Jesus as the Lord and the Son of God. On the other hand, there is no reason to deny that the apostles passed on to their listeners what was really said and done by the Lord with that fuller understanding which they enjoyed,[14] having been instructed by the glorious events of the

---

7. Lk 1:2; Acts 1:21–22.
8. Lk 24:28; Jn 15:27; Acts 1:8; 10:39; 13:31.
9. Lk 24:44–48; Acts 2:32; 3:15; 5:30–32.
10. Acts 10:36–41.
11. Compare Acts 13:16–41 with Acts 17:22–31.
12. Acts 2:36; Jn 20:28.
13. Acts 2:22; 10:37–39.
14. Jn 2:22; 12:16; 11:51–52; cf. 14:26; 16:12–13; 7:39.

Christ and taught by the light of the Spirit of truth.[15] So, just as Jesus himself after his resurrection "interpreted to them"[16] the words of the Old Testament as well as his own,[17] they too interpreted his words and deeds according to the needs of their listeners. "Devoting themselves to the ministry of the word,"[18] they preached and made use of various modes of speaking which were suited to their own purpose and the mentality of their listeners. For they were debtors[19] "to Greeks and barbarians, to the wise and the foolish."[20] But these modes of speaking with which the preachers proclaimed Christ must be distinguished and (properly) assessed: catecheses, stories, testimonia, hymns, doxologies, prayers, and other literary forms of this sort which were in sacred scripture and were accustomed to be used by people of that time.

IX. This primitive instruction, which was at first passed on by word of mouth and then in writing, for it soon happened that many tried "to compile a narrative of the things"[21] which concerned the Lord Jesus, was committed to writing by the sacred authors in four gospels for the benefit of the churches, with a method suited to the peculiar purpose which each (author) set for himself. From the many things handed down they selected some things, reduced others to a synthesis, (still) others they explicated as they kept in mind the situation of the churches. With every (possible) means they sought that their readers might become aware of the reliability[22] of those words by which they had been instructed. Indeed, from what they had received the sacred writers above all selected the things which

---

15. Jn 14:26; 16:13.
16. Lk 24:27.
17. Lk 24:44–45; Acts 1:3.
18. Acts 6:4.
19. 1 Cor 9:19–23.
20. Rom 1:14.
21. Lk 1:1.
22. Lk 1:4.

were suited to the various situations of the faithful and to the purpose which they had in mind, and adapted their narration of them to the same situations and purpose. Since the meaning of a statement also depends on the sequence, the evangelists, in passing on the words and deeds of our savior, explained these now in one context, now in another, depending on (their) usefulness to the readers. Consequently, let the exegete seek out the meaning intended by the evangelist in narrating a saying or a deed in a certain way or in placing it in a certain context. For the truth of the story is not at all affected by the fact that the evangelists relate the words and deeds of the Lord in a different order,[23] and express his sayings not literally but differently, while preserving (their) sense.[24] For, as St. Augustine says, "It is quite probable that each evangelist believed it to have been his duty to recount what he had to in that order in which it pleased God to suggest it to his memory, in those things at least in which the order, whether it be this or that, detracts in nothing from the truth and authority of the gospel. But why the Holy Spirit, who apportions individually to each one as he wills,[25] and who therefore undoubtedly also governed and ruled the minds of the holy (writers) in recalling what they were to write because of the preeminent authority which the books were to enjoy, permitted one to compile his narrative in this way, and another in that, anyone with pious diligence may seek the reason and with divine aid will be able to find it."[26]

X. Unless the exegete pays attention to all these things which pertain to the origin and composition of the gospels and makes proper use of all the laudable achievements of recent research, he will not fulfill his task of probing into what the sacred writers in-

---

23. See John Chrysostom, *Hom. in Matth.* 1, 3 (PG 57. 16–17).

24. Augustine, *De consensu evangelistarum* 2.12, 28 (PL 34. 1090–91; CSEL 43. 127–29).

25. 1 Cor 12:11.

26. *De consensu evangelistarum* 2.21, 51–52 (PL 34. 1102; CSEL 43. 153).

tended and what they really said. From the results of the new investigations it is apparent that the doctrine and the life of Jesus were not simply reported for the sole purpose of being remembered, but were "preached" so as to offer the church a basis of faith and of morals. The interpreter (then), by tirelessly scrutinizing the testimony of the evangelists, will be able to illustrate more profoundly the perennial theological value of the gospels and bring out clearly how necessary and important the church's interpretation is.

XI. There are still many things, and of the greatest importance, in the discussion and explanation of which the Catholic exegete can and must freely exercise his skill and genius so that each may contribute his part to the advantage of all, to the continued progress of sacred doctrine, to the preparation and further support of the judgment to be exercised by the ecclesiastical magisterium, and to the defense and honor of the church.[27] But let him always be disposed to obey the magisterium of the church and not forget that the apostles, filled with the Holy Spirit, preached the good news, and that the gospels were written under the inspiration of the Holy Spirit, who preserved their authors from all error. "Now we have not learned of the plan of our salvation from any others than those through whom the gospel has come to us. Indeed, what they once preached they later passed on to us in the scriptures by the will of God, as the ground and pillar of our faith. It is not right to say that they preached before they had acquired perfect knowledge, as some would venture to say who boast of being correctors of the apostles. In fact, after our Lord rose from the dead and they were invested with power from on high, as the Holy Spirit came down upon them, they were filled with all (his gifts) and had perfect knowledge. They went forth to the ends of the earth, one and all with God's gospel, announcing the news of God's bounty to us and proclaiming heavenly peace to men."[28]

---

27. *DaS* 47 (*AAS* 35 [1943] 319; *EnchBib* §565; *RSS,* 102).
28. Irenaeus, *Adversus haereses* 3.1, 1 (Harvey 2.2; PG 7. 844).

XII. 3. Those whose *task it is to teach in seminaries and similar institutions* should have it as their "prime concern that . . . Holy Scripture be so taught as both the dignity of the discipline and the needs of the times require."[29] Let teachers above all explain its theological teaching so that the sacred scriptures "may become for the future priests of the church both a pure and never-failing source for their own spiritual life, as well as food and strength for the sacred task of preaching which they are about to undertake."[30] When they practice the art of criticism, especially so-called literary criticism, let them not pursue it as an end in itself, but that through it they might more plainly perceive the sense intended by God through the sacred writer. Let them not stop, therefore, halfway, content only with their literary discoveries, but show in addition how these things really contribute to a clearer understanding of revealed doctrine or, if it be the case, to the refutation of errors. Instructors who follow these norms will enable their students to find in sacred scripture that which can "raise the minds to God, nourish the soul, and further the interior life."[31]

XIII. 4. Those who *instruct the Christian people in sacred sermons* have need of great prudence. Let them above all pass on doctrine, mindful of St. Paul's warning: "Look to yourself and your teaching; hold on to that. For by so doing you will save both yourself and those who listen to you."[32] They are to refrain entirely from proposing idle or insufficiently established novelties. As for new opinions already solidly established, they may explain them, if need be, but with caution and due care for their listeners. When they narrate biblical events, let them not add imaginative details which are not consonant with the truth.

---

29. Apostolic Letter, *Quoniam in re biblica* (*EnchBib* §162; *RSS*, 36).
30. *DaS* 55 (*AAS* 35 [1943] 322; *EnchBib* §567; *RSS*, 104).
31. *DaS* 25 (*AAS* 35 [1943] 311; *EnchBib* §552; *RSS*, 93).
32. 1 Tim 4:16.

XIV. This virtue of prudence should be cherished especially by *those who publish for the faithful.* Let them carefully bring forth the heavenly riches of the divine word "that the faithful . . . may be moved and inflamed rightly to conform their lives (to them)."[33] They should consider it a sacred duty never to depart in the slightest degree from the common doctrine and tradition of the church. They should indeed exploit all the real advances of biblical science which the diligence of recent (students) has produced. But they are to avoid entirely the rash remarks of innovators.[34] They are strictly forbidden to disseminate, led on by some pernicious itch for novelty, any trial solutions for difficulties without a prudent selection and serious discrimination, for thus they disturb the faith of many.

XV. This Pontifical Biblical Commission has already considered it proper to recall that books and articles in magazines and newspapers on biblical subjects are subject to the authority and jurisdiction of ordinaries, since they treat of religious matters and pertain to the religious instruction of the faithful.[35] Ordinaries are therefore requested to keep watch with great care over popular writings of this sort.

XVI. 5. Those who are in charge of biblical associations are to comply faithfully with the norms laid down by the Pontifical Biblical Commission.[36]

XVII. If all these things are observed, the study of the sacred scriptures will contribute to the benefit of the faithful. Even in our time everyone realizes the wisdom of what St. Paul wrote: The

---

33. *DaS* 50 (*AAS* 35 [1943] 320; *EnchBib* §566; *RSS,* 103).

34. Apostolic Letter *Quoniam in re biblica* 13 (*EnchBib* §175; *RSS,* 38).

35. Instruction *De consociationibus biblicis . . .* (*AAS* 48 [1956] 63; *EnchBib* §626).

36. Ibid. (*EnchBib* §622–33).

sacred writings "can instruct (us) for salvation through faith in Christ Jesus. All scripture is divinely inspired and profitable for teaching, for reproof, for correction, and for training in uprightness, so that the man of God may be perfect, equipped for every good work."[37]

XVIII. The holy father, Pope Paul VI, at the audience graciously granted to the undersigned secretary on 21 April 1964, approved this Instruction and ordered the publication of it.

Rome, 21 April 1964   *Secretary of the Commission*
                                 Benjamin N. Wambacq, O.Praem.

---

37. 2 Tim 3:15–17.

3.

Vatican Council II
Dogmatic Constitution, *Dei Verbum* §19
(*AAS* 58 [1966] 826–27)

Holy mother the church has firmly and with utmost constancy held, and continues to hold, that the four gospels just named, whose historical character the church unhesitatingly asserts, faithfully hand on what Jesus the Son of God, while living among men, really did and taught for their eternal salvation until the day he was taken up into heaven (see Acts 1:1–2). Indeed, after the ascension of the Lord the apostles handed on to their hearers what he had said and done. This they did with that clearer understanding which they enjoyed[1] after they had been instructed by the events of Christ's risen life [*eventibus gloriosis Christi instructi*] and taught by the light of the Spirit of truth.[2] The sacred authors, however, wrote the four gospels, selecting some things from the many which had been handed on either by word of mouth or in writing, reducing some of them to a synthesis, explicating [*explanantes* (see Instruction, par. IX)] some things in view of the situation of their churches, and preserving the form of proclamation but always in such fashion that they recounted to us the honest truth about Jesus [*vera et sincera de Iesu*].[3] For their intention in writing was that either from their own

---

1. See Jn 2:22; 12:16; cf. 14:26; 16:12–13; 7:39.

2. See Jn 14:26; 16:13.

3. See the Instruction *Sancta Mater Ecclesia* issued by the Pontifical Commission for the Promotion of Biblical Studies (*AAS* 56 [1964] 712–18, esp. p. 715). Cf. DS §3999b–e. *Sancta Mater Ecclesia* are the first three Latin words with which the Biblical Commission's Instruction begins. Note that "vera et sincera de Iesu" cannot be simply equated with historical truth; see n. 41 in the commentary on the Instruction.

memory and recollections, or from the testimony of those who themselves "from the beginning were eyewitnesses and ministers of the word," we might know "the truth" [*veritatem* (cf. Vulgate version)] concerning those matters about which we have been instructed (cf. Lk 1:2–4).[4]

---

4. In studying this paragraph from Vatican Council II, one must remember that it was the product of much conservative and enlightened debate as *Dei verbum* took shape. The struggle between the two groups of council fathers can still be seen in the contrast in par. 19 between the unhesitating assertion of the "historical character" of the gospels and the later nuanced explanation of what the "sacred authors" have passed on to us. This explanation uses phrases derived from the Instruction itself. For a proper understanding of par. 19 and also of par. 11 on inerrancy, one should consult above all A. Grillmeier, "The Divine Inspiration and the Interpretation of Sacred Scripture" (n. 41 above), 204–15 (especially the details about Form F). Unfortunately, the debate about inerrancy (especially the remarks of Cardinal König and others) has been completely glossed over by such an important council father as A. Cardinal Bea in his comments on *Dei Verbum* in *The Word of God and Mankind* (Chicago: Franciscan Herald Press, 1967) 184–91. What Bea has written there has to be taken with a grain of salt; it has to yield to what is otherwise known about the council debate itself.

SELECT BIBLIOGRAPHY

Achtemeier, P.J., *The Inspiration of Scripture: Problems and Proposals* (Philadelphia, PA: Westminster, 1980).

Brown, R.E., *The Critical Meaning of the Bible* (New York, NY: Paulist, 1981).

———, *Jesus God and Man: Modern Biblical Reflections* (Milwaukee, WI: Bruce, 1967).

———, " 'Who Do Men Say That I Am?'—A Survey of Modern Scholarship on Gospel Christology," *Biblical Reflections on Crises Facing the Church* (New York, NY: Paulist, 1975) 20–37.

Conzelmann, H., *Jesus* (Philadelphia, PA: Fortress, 1978).

Dunn, J.D.G., *Christology in the Making: A New Testament Inquiry into the Origins of the Doctrine of the Incarnation* (Philadelphia, PA: Westminster, 1980).

———, *The Evidence of Jesus* (Philadelphia, PA: Westminster, 1985).

Fuller, R.H. and P. Perkins, *Who Is This Christ? Gospel Christology and Contemporary Faith* (Philadelphia, PA: Fortress, 1983).

International Theological Commission, *Select Questions on Christology: September 1980* (Washington, DC: United States Catholic Conference, 1980).

Johnson, E.A., *Consider Jesus: Waves of Renewal in Christology* (New York, NY: Crossroad, 1990).

Kingsbury, J.D., *Jesus Christ in Matthew, Mark, and Luke* (Philadelphia, PA: Fortress, 1981).

McEleney, N.J., *The Growth of the Gospels* (New York, NY: Paulist, 1979).

Marrow, S.B., *The Words of Jesus in Our Gospels: A Catholic Response to Fundamentalism* (New York, NY: Paulist, 1979).

Meier, J.P., *A Marginal Jew: Rethinking the Historical Jesus* (2 vols.; New York: Doubleday, 1991, 199?).

O'Collins, G., *What Are They Saying About Jesus?* (New York, NY: Paulist, 1977).

Perkins, P., *Resurrection: New Testament Witness and Contemporary Reflection* (Garden City, NY: Doubleday, 1984).

N.B. A still more positive image of the Biblical Commission can be seen in its recent publications: (1) *Fede e cultura alla luce della Bibbia: Atti della sessione plenaria 1979 della Pontificia Commissione Biblica* (Turin: Editrice Elle di Ci, 1981). It contains an address of Pope John Paul II to the members of the Commission (26 April 1979) and fifteen articles in various languages (English, French, German, Italian, Latin, and Spanish), written by members of the Commission, and introduced by J.-D. Barthélemy. (2) *Bible et christologie* (Paris: Cerf, 1984). It contains a common statement and nine so-called commentaries, essays on christological topics written by individual members of the Commission and published on their own authority. The preface is written by the secretary, Henri Cazelles, P.S.S. [See my English translation, *Scripture and Christology: A Statement of the Biblical Commission with a Commentary* (New York, NY/Mahwah, NJ: Paulist, 1985).] (3) *Unité et diversité dans l'Eglise: Texte officiel de la Commission Biblique Pontificale et travaux personnels des membres* (Vatican City: Libreria Editrice Vaticana, 1989). It is introduced by a preface written by the secretary, Henri Cazelles, P.S.S.

INDEXES

1.

Biblical Index

2.

Index of Modern Authors

3.

Topical Index